PILGRIMS' FOOTSTEPS REVISITED

BERT SLADER

*A walk along the Ancient Road
to Santiago de Compostela*

For Padraig,
with very best wishes
Bert Slader Dec 99

QUEST BOOKS

First published in 1989 as Pilgrims' Footsteps
by Quest Books (NI)
2 Slievenabrock Avenue, Newcastle, Co. Down BT33 OHZ

Reprinted 1990

New extended edition published in 1999 as Pilgrims' Footsteps Revisited

Printed in Ireland by ColourBooks Ltd.

A CIP catalogue of this book is available from the British Library

ISBN 1-872027-10-5 (a revised and extended edition of 1-872027-00-8 first edition)

**This revised and extended edition retitled
Pilgrims' Footsteps Revisited
is published to mark
the 10th annual MS Ireland Walk to Santiago
originally inspired by Pilgrims' Footsteps.**

Cover Photographs:
The Pilgrims' Bridge, Puente la Reina
Insert: MS Walkers under the bridge

Illustrations by the author
Photographs by the author and MS Society

Contents

Chapter		Page
1	BEYOND THE BLACK MOUNTAIN.................	1
2	THE RIGHT MOMENT.................................	3
3	A JOURNEY BACK THROUGH TIME................	15
4	ESTELLA LA BELLA....................................	23
5	CHAOS AND ORDER....................................	31
6	BRUNO: THE REAL PILGRIM.........................	40
7	BURGOS..	51
8	THE THREE FRENCH GENTLEMEN................	63
9	THE BELGIAN BOYS WALK TO FREEDOM......	84
10	LEON: CITY OF LIGHT................................	97
11	THE GIRL WITH THE ALMOND EYES..............	107
12	THE WILD DOGS OF FONCEBADON...............	114
13	THE KNIGHTS TEMPLAR: PROTECTORS OF THE ROAD..	129
14	O CEBREIRO: A VILLAGE IN THE CLOUDS.......	137
15	THE LANES OF ENCHANTMENT....................	144
16	THE LAST STAGE.......................................	155
17	THE PILGRIM CITY.....................................	169
APPENDIX 1		
	MS WALKS TO SANTIAGO..............................	178

For

FAE, BEN *and* **KATIE**

And all who have walked the Camino de Santiago for MS over the
past 10 years.

Acknowledgements

My thanks are due to the many friends who gave me encouragement, support and practical help. They are also due to those I met on the journey, the local people who helped me on my way, the Three French Gentlemen, the young men from Belgium and Bruno, the real pilgrim.

Walter Starkie, through the story of his own journeys, The Road To Santiago, was my guide and mentor. It was his inspiration which set me on the Road.

PILGRIMS' FOOTSTEPS BECOMES PILGRIMS' FOOTSTEPS REVISITED

When I set out on my own from St. Jean Pied-de Port in June 1985 to walk to Santiago de Compostela, I could have had no idea that it was the beginning of the most interesting and fulfilling stage in my life.

The walk itself led to a book, to lectures and a number of series of radio talks called 'A Traveller's Tales'. Shortly after Pilgrims' Footsteps was first published, I had a phone call from Lorna Mitchell of the Multiple Sclerosis Society of Ireland. Donncha O'Dulaing had found a copy of the book in the offices of RTÉ, she told me, and they were considering the Road to Santiago as their next fund-raising walk.

Lorna and Donncha came to see me in Newcastle, County Down and I helped them plan their route by suggesting ten one-day walks from the thirty-odd stages to Santiago. Donncha recorded an interview with me about my own walk for his Sunday programme on RTÉ and I wished them well.

The walk was a wonderful success and some sixty walkers raised a considerable sum for MS in Ireland. The Society gained a new group of friends and allies. Public awareness of MS was greatly increased through press and radio coverage.

Later that year I had another phone call from Lorna. This time she was not asking for advice. We met on neutral ground in Dundalk. "They're a grand crowd," she said persuasively, "Super people. Great craic." She wanted me to lead the walk next year. I offered advice and encouragement. I bobbed and weaved like a boxer trying to stay out of trouble. It was no use. She wasn't listening.

It was time to come clean. It meant telling her, that having led groups at home and abroad all my adult life, I felt I had done my bit. All that was yesterday and a little voice had whispered in my ear, "Never Again". It was someone else's turn.

Lorna wasn't listening. With great patience she reminded me that it had been 'Pilgrims' Footsteps' which had inspired the first walk. She told me of the huge effort the walkers made to raise funds for MS supporting
the work of the Society. Anything I might do as a leader seemed very small in comparison.

She neglected to tell me about the aggravations. The fast crowd who were afraid to pause to look at the day in case their feet would take root. The mimics who thought that the Ulster accent was a special gift from St. James himself. The experts on every topic, Irish or Spanish, sport or wine, food or photography.

And then a few years later there was the prankster who, having used an associate to set me off on a tirade against mobile phones earlier in the day, had to hunt in his rucksack for his own ringing mobile. He reached it to me, announcing loudly "it's for you Bert!" It was a joke phone, of course, purchased with this coup in mind.

That first year I went with the group, we started at the end of May, at the statue of the pilgrim outside Puente la Reina. There were sixty-four of us from Ireland, North and South, from every corner of the island. We had ten one-day stages of the Camino de Santiago in front of us. I looked them over. They were wearing MS tee-shirts and shorts, with trainers or boots. They scampered about taking photographs, smiling at me trustingly.

Noreen stepped up to the statue and said a prayer for a safe journey. And then we were on our way, laughing and talking, cheerfully, nervously. These were the first steps. There was a long way to go but I felt we would make it to the end. We would all make it to Santiago.

This year we are going back on the 10th annual walk to Santiago and many who have walked with us before come back to walk again and again.

In a life-time of travel and mountaineering in some of the world's most fascinating places, these journeys to Santiago with my MS walking friends have been the most interesting and fulfilling of all.

This new edition of Pilgrims' Footstep is called **'Pilgrims' Footsteps Revisited'** to mark this 10th Annual MS walk to Santiago and it has been my very great privilege to have been associated with all those who have walked for M.S.

Bert Slader

CHAPTER 1

Beyond the Black Mountain

At that exciting moment when the decision is made to make something of one's life, the chances are that the process has already begun.

For some the quest may be through contemplation, study or conversation with like minds. Others will use the practical experiences of life to help them on the way. There will be those who need to set out on an actual journey, flying off to the shrines at Jerusalem or Lourdes, or to see the treasures or wonders of the world. A few may travel on foot like the medieval pilgrims, following in their footsteps.

My journey began as a schoolboy's adventure on the Black Mountain above Belfast. Six of us in our early teens climbed the hill from our homes in the city. It was a prize beyond expectation. The achievement of climbing our first mountain was important but the real thrill was to be in this particular place and to see our world below us.

For the first time we could look down on the city and the surrounding countryside laid out like a gigantic map. We turned to take in the whole of this new horizon and could see the coasts and hills of Antrim and Down, Lough Neagh, the biggest lake in the British Isles, and the mountains of Mourne and Donegal.

There and then we decided to cycle around our country, camping on the way, passing through all five counties that were in view.

It was just after the end of the last World War and rationing was still strictly in force but that was not our greatest problem. Most of the mothers thought the expedition foolhardy and in the event only two of us were allowed to go.

It was a journey of over two hundred miles and took four long days. We met great country kindness, lost the bread coupons and discovered what it meant to be leg-weary and saddle-sore. We learned a little of the art of camping, were fascinated by the different landscapes of our own small country and were told a blatant lie by a man of the cloth.

On the final day we burst a tyre and, with bicycle parts so scarce, were unable to buy a replacement. It meant that we had to take the train for the last twenty miles to Belfast and then walk the five miles from the railway station to our homes.

But there was no disappointment in not being able to complete the trip by bicycle. We were elated but found it impossible to explain to our friends and families why we had enjoyed the journey so much. It was hard for them to understand that it was not because of the distance covered or the difficulties overcome. Our reward was simply to have been on the journey.

Other expeditions, often on foot in high mountains, in Europe, the Arctic and the Himalayas led me along the road of the quest and sometimes, it has to be said, diverted me from it. Then circumstances directed me to one particular route, the ancient pilgrims' road to Santiago de Compostela. It was clear then that I should follow in the footsteps of those pilgrims.

At that sublime moment when the decision is made to set out in search of the holy grail of enlightenment the journey has already begun, in this instance on the Black Mountain which watches over Belfast.

CHAPTER 2

The Right Moment

Out of the heat haze the jumbled line of black rock and snow peaks of the Pyrenees emerged in the middle distance.

From the flight deck of the aircraft we seemed to be gliding slowly earthwards, almost hanging in the sky; and, as if to break me in gently to the idea of travelling alone, I was the only passenger on the flight from Dublin. A party of Irish pilgrims booked to fly to Lourdes had cancelled at the last moment but the aircraft had to make the trip to collect a returning group. I had been invited to the flight deck for take-off and landing and as we descended I fancied I could see the line of my walking route across the mountains.

The pass over the Pyrenees was to be the first stage of a journey on foot along the ancient pilgrim road to Santiago de Compostela in North-West Spain. My intention was to try to find the old route and to follow in the footsteps of those who had travelled it over the past one thousand years.

A journey worth doing deserves a worthy starting point and mine had been an obvious choice. St. Jean Pied-de-Port is one of the most attractive and interesting towns on the French side of the Pyrenees. The Romans maintained an important camp nearby and used it as a staging post for the difficult journey across the mountains. For many centuries it was fortified and its ancient houses, shops and church are packed neatly along narrow streets within immense walls.

On the way to St. Jean by the early morning mountain train I shared a compartment with a school party on a day's outing. We pulled up through the foothills by wooded valleys and climbed a gorge beside a mountain torrent. My companions ignored the view and concentrated on teasing and annoying each other. They opened cans of soft drinks and ate the food they had brought for lunch. They fidgeted and pushed each other's elbows and changed seats as if involved in some hectic game. We arrived at St. Jean at nine o'clock before the town had come to life. As the train slowed to walking pace the young people burst from its doors heading for the shops with their teachers in hot pursuit. They left a silence behind them on the platform and I would have to admit to being as excited as they were at the beginning of this particular day.

It is possible to drive across the Pyrenees by a modern road from St. Jean in France to Roncesvalles in Spain but the pilgrim track followed a higher route over a mountain pass further to the east and this was to be the first stage of my journey.

As the shops opened I bought the essentials for the day, fresh bread, fruit, garlic sausage and a small round of goat cheese. It looked more than enough but experience teaches the walker not to estimate the needs of the day on the basis of the after-breakfast appetite. At the edge of the town I filled two water bottles at a public tap and set off for the frontier ridge.

Even with the prospect of eight hundred and fifty kilometres ahead of me it was easy to make an optimistic start. It would be four or five hours of good walking to the first objective, the crest of the Pyrenees, but the day was fine and, like the wish in the old Irish blessing, the road was rising before me. Another traveller had set out along The Road to Santiago.

The step out of the shadow of the peak, into the sunlight and across the pass was the point of no return. In ten paces France was left behind. It was too late for a last look at the ordered picturesque of the French countryside. All that, like life's experience to this moment, was now behind the ridge and slipping into the back of the mind.

To the south was a huge spread of Spanish landscape held in the glare of the afternoon sun. Miles away, below the forests of the slopes and beyond the foothills, the heat haze faded the earth into the bottom of the sky.

Almost one thousand years ago this pass became one of the two main routes across the Pyrenees used by pilgrims on the way to the shrine of St. James at Santiago. It was the more difficult of the crossings by reason of the physical effort required and the danger of attack by wild animals and robbers and was therefore the more highly regarded. My hope was that it would still be possible to follow the old route from this pass down through Navarre, across the out-rider ranges of the Cantabrian Mountains, eventually crossing that range into the Province of Galicia to reach Santiago near the Atlantic coast.

The Cult of St. James, Santiago in Spanish, is based on the belief that James the Apostle visited Spain between 38 and 40 A.D. He is reputed to have landed in Andalucia in the south-east of the country and journeyed north using the Roman roads to the village of Padron at the mouth of the River Ulla on the north-west coast.

His travels and preaching took some years and in Zaragoza he witnessed the miracle now venerated in that city as the Virgin of the Pillar. When James returned to Judaea he was beheaded on the orders of King Herod in the year 44 A.D. Two of his disciples are believed to have rescued his body from the dogs outside the walls of Jerusalem and sailed with it from the port of Jaffa through the Mediterranean and along the west coast of Iberia to return to the River Ulla and Padron. The story records that the journey took only seven days and the stone to which, by tradition, the boat was moored, is still to be seen there under the church altar. The body was buried in a stone coffin some distance inland at a point where the oxen pulling the cart stopped. The crypt was covered with a vaulted roof and a small church erected over the grave. Some years later the two disciples died and were buried on the same site.

As the centuries passed the tomb was concealed with rocks and bushes as the countryside was over-run by the Visigoths and the Moors. The area became over-grown and the site forgotten.

In the ninth century a hermit called Palagio, one of many living in the district, guided the Bishop of Iria to the tomb. The Bishop immediately recognised it as that of St. James. The King, Alphonso 11, visited the crypt and provided funds to build a church and a monastery for an abbot and twelve monks. The place became known as Santiago de Compostela and attracted pilgrims from the surrounding area and further afield in Spain.

The first foreign pilgrims arrived from France in 950 A.D. led by Bishop Gottschalf. Their route came to be called the Camino Francés, the road of the foreigners or the French and, as it was followed by an increasing number of people, it became one of the most significant spiritual and cultural links in Western Europe.

The great Benedictine Abbey of Cluny began to stimulate devotion to St. James as a symbol of Christendom. The Order founded priories, rest houses and hospitals along the route and other orders added to this provision for travellers. The Church ensured that the pilgrims were properly organised and received in the towns and villages along the route. The Knights Templar provided protection in the most dangerous areas. A scallop shell was worn as the pilgrim's badge and on his return a pilgrim could add this device to his coat of arms. Over the years the cockle shell was sometimes referred to as the emblem but this confusion may simply have arisen because the French word for scallop, coquille.

Suitable footwear was recommended by the authorities, as was the wearing of a special style of cloak which would give protection from the weather during the day and act as a warm blanket at night. Other items of equipment which were advised were a gourd for water or wine and a stout staff longer than a man's height. This was to be used for defence against robbers, dogs or wild animals and to assist the pilgrim on difficult ground.

In the twelfth century a French cleric called Amery Picaud of Poitou collected the information available on the pilgrimage and its route and produced what was perhaps the world's first tourist guide. It was called the Codex Calixtinus after the Pope of the day, Calixtus 11. The Codex followed the route through France over the Pyrenees and across the width of Spain to Santiago giving advice on the accommodation, wine, water and food and offering opinions on the people of each area. Near home Picaud describes the men as being fine warriors, full of vigour and courage, elegant, handsome, spiritual, well-mannered and hospitable. Was he perhaps trying to ensure that he would be able to return home after his travels?

In Gascony he found the people empty-headed and verbose. He liked the wine of Bordeaux but not the people and described Les Landes as a desolate land lacking bread, wine and meat. His most scathing criticism was reserved for the people of the Pyrenees, on both sides of that range. A great deal has changed in 850 years but the line of the route, as detailed by Picaud, is still regarded as the authentic pilgrimage and this was the route I hoped to follow. His advice on where to find good food and wine proved to be still remarkably appropriate. There have been changes which make the journey easier for the traveller on foot as well as some which make it worse but even Picaud would be pleased now by the people of the Pyrenees.

The pilgrimage was at its most popular in the eleventh and twelfth centuries and some sources estimate that between ½ million and 1 million pilgrims made the journey each year. Given the much smaller population of Europe at that time such figures are hard to accept as credible but the records do show that Santiago de Compostela and the tomb of St. James reached a position of the greatest significance in the Christian world.

The would-be traveller on a pilgrimage, or on any other sort of major journey not undertaken out of the essentials of business or daily living, has to face the question "Why?" as well as those of "Where? When?" and "How? In the case of a pilgrimage the reason is usually an act of religious piety focused on a cult or a shrine. There are other reasons, however, which may not be always so readily explained. They may only appear once the venture is underway. These hidden reasons must have influenced the historical development of particular pilgrimages.

Chaucer depicted the pilgrimage to Canterbury as a pleasant, interesting adventure to be travelled in holiday mood, with the pilgrims entertaining each other as they journeyed through the delightful Kentish countryside in Spring. The tales were told by those who had experienced life and were full of intrigue, excitement, and bawdy good humour. None more so than the adventures of the Wife of Bath who had been on seven pilgrimages including three to Jerusalem and, on one occasion, to Santiago "in Galice at seint Jame"

Although pilgrims, on foot or on horse-back, often covered long distances in a day on the way to Santiago few seemed to be in a hurry to reach their destination. Some took days or weeks off the main route to visit a monastery or shrine. Others lingered at the most hospitable locations. Like Chaucer's pilgrims they clearly enjoyed the travelling in spite of the hardship, danger and the physical effort.

Some years ago, at the end of a journey through the Pyrenees, I decided to finish by crossing the range from Spain to France. I had heard of the Pilgrim Road to Santiago but knew little of its history or religious significance.

When I reached the beech woods above the Spanish village of Roncesvalles they were dappled by a thin, white, early-morning mist. At this height the first rays of the sun are from below the horizontal. They made shafts of light through the vapour and between the branches. It was not yet warm enough for the heat to disperse the mist and I could only see the path in snatches. The light flickered on the eddies and, from this unusual angle, played eerie tricks amongst the trees.

I realised then that I was retracing the route of the Road to Santiago. Pilgrims coming in the opposite direction, up the long steep climb from France, would have rested here on a hot afternoon. Some, finding the distance and the ascent hard going, might well have sheltered here for the night and walked down to Roncesvalles in the morning. Many hundreds of thousands would have followed this path. The very fact that so many had passed this way and the strange atmospheric light gave the place a mystical aura strong enough to stop me in my tracks.

Above the woods I reached the main ridge and saw the French foothills and valleys. From the pass I could see a track taking the best route down. It was wide enough for a horseman to pass a traveller on foot and in places worn into the hillside to the depth of a metre. This had to be the Roman road from St. Jean Pied-de-Port to Spain which in its turn, a thousand years later, was used by the pilgrims as their route across the Pyrenees.

That evening in a small restaurant against the walls of St. Jean I ordered the dish of the region. Madame brought me Coquilles St. Jacques and explained that the dish had been invented in St. Jean to celebrate the scallop shell emblem of the Santiago pilgrim.

Later I read an account by Walter Starkie, Irish writer and diplomat, who had made the pilgrimage to Santiago four times. His story of the

THE FOUR ROADS
TO SANTIAGO

BAY OF
BISCAY

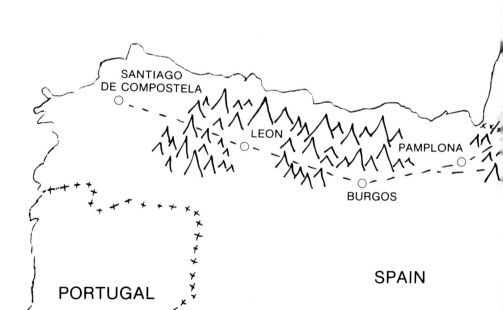

SANTIAGO
DE COMPOSTELA

LEON

PAMPLONA

BURGOS

SPAIN

PORTUGAL

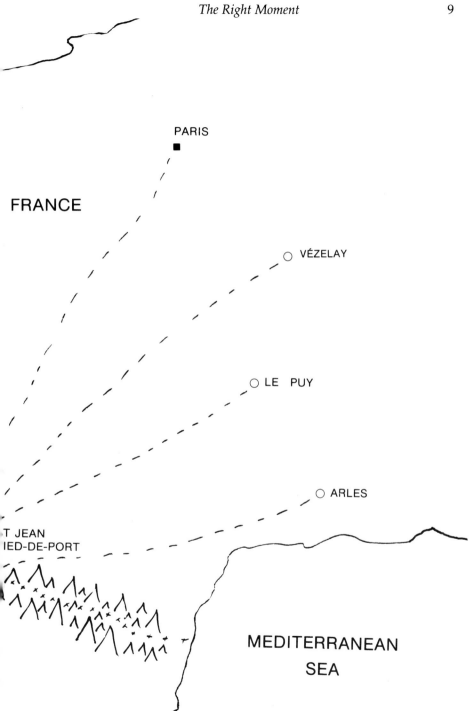

journey, a true wanderer's tale, the mystical beech woods above Roncesvalles and the track near the pass were sufficient. It only needed the right moment.

Sometimes, although such moments are rare, we arrive at a point in life where it is possible for us to decide for ourselves on the next step. Having chosen to undertake a pilgrimage the medieval traveller had picked a difficult road. Such a journey was known to be long, hard and dangerous but it was a choice away from the usual rhythm of life. There might be hardship, physical exhaustion and risk to life and limb but there would be also comradeship, the interest of new places, hospitality and the opportunity to earn spiritual grace.

Having reached the frontier ridge between France and Spain on my own journey to Santiago I stopped to eat in the early afternoon. I spread out the food and gear around me and leaned back against a rock to look at the day. Surprisingly it was not a time to rest pleasantly in the sunshine. For the first time in many years of travel, including other solo journeys in this range of mountains, I felt lonely. It must have been because there was so much to share and no one to share it with. I ate a little, rested briefly and was soon on my way. As I started to walk the loneliness vanished, as if it was right to be travelling on my own.

On the way down, and with time to spare, I looked for traces of the old route. The Spanish side of the mountains is a complex of steep, wooded valleys and rocky peaks. I crossed a rise and came upon a flock of large birds. They were neatly arranged on the slope, all pointing the same way, rumps towards me like earnest delegates at a conference waiting for the celebrated speaker to appear. They were big and plump, speckled, greyish-brown in colour. They had the look of birds of prey who had fed well and were now resting. Could it be that they were vultures? I had often watched these great birds in the mountains circling above me as if waiting for some accident to happen. But I had never seen them at their ease. When they sensed my presence they stirred themselves slowly and, in their own good time, rose on huge wings and soared away.

It was through this tactically difficult terrain that Charlmagne returned from a foray into Spain in the eight century. Here his rearguard under the command of Count Roland was massacred by the Basques in revenge for the raid. The Song of Roland commemorates the event and, in medieval times, minstrels used the song to encourage the pilgrims on this long and arduous stage of their journey to Santiago.

My explorations and musings led me down on the wrong side of the final ridge and it was early evening when I reached Roncesvalles. The collegiate church is Gothic and was an important stopping place for pilgrims. A few kilometres further is Burgete and I decided that this would be far enough for the first day.

There were two inns in the village, one on either side of the road, almost facing each other. I chose the one on the right hand side and entered a spacious hall. It was panelled in dark wood with glazed, net-curtained doors, elegant glass lamp shades and highly-polished antique furniture. There was no reception desk nor was there a bell to ring for attention. The whole building was so quiet and still that it seemed completely empty.

As I was about to leave, to try the other inn, a girl appeared from the inner recesses and seemed pleased to be able to offer me a room and dinner. The bedroom was on the first floor, one of a number around the sides of a large landing with a bare, polished wooden floor. The room was furnished in old fashioned style with a high, draped bed, soft mattress and furniture made to last. At ceiling height were metal tension rods, carefully and reassuringly placed to keep the walls apart. Years ago this room had been designed for the traveller's comfort and it was still able to fulfil that function with style. I unpacked my rucksack on the coverlet and showered in the bathroom across the landing.

I came down for dinner at eight thirty and as I reached the last few stairs the girl appeared as if she had been waiting for me to descend. She showed me into a small dining room with an antique dresser along one wall apparently made to fit its length. Plates perched on its shelves, ready for use, each one looking like a collector's item.

One table was laid with a stiff, white cloth and a freshly starched white napkin. It was the only table with a basket of bread and a jug of wine and I knew then that I would be the only one to dinner.

The soup came in a large tureen, clear and with a delicious tang of onions. I prepared to do the broth justice with the appetite of a long day in the mountain air but as I lifted the spoon the loneliness of mid-day returned in a great pang and took away the hunger.

Outside the curtained window a vehicle rumbled past and I heard people chattering happily as they walked down the street. Inside the inn there was total silence. This dining room, and indeed the whole building represented a graceful past. They still functioned effectively, providing comfortable lodging and good food. But what had happened to the people? It was a quietness that seemed to stop time. Everything was as it had been but for the absence of the bustle of staff and customers. Only the girl, now presumably washing pots in the kitchen, and the solitary traveller were left to keep it working.

I drank a draught of the wine as a toast to the inn's past and it broke the spell of melancholy. It tasted as red wine should, strong and dry. The door opened and the girl came in bringing lamb chops and new potatoes and to check that all was well.

It was now. The dark moment had passed and my appetite had returned. I set about the meal with gusto and it pleased the girl to see me enjoying the food and wine.

The bed was big enough to allow me to stretch out in every direction and I eased my tired feet and legs hoping a night's rest would bring back their energy. The front door of the inn slammed shut as the girl left for her home elsewhere in the village. I had the inn to myself. It was reassuring to settle back on the pillows knowing that this was the right place to spend the first night on the Road to Santiago.

Next morning a lane behind the inn led to a track through farmland and forest and, after a couple of hours, I came out on the road near the village of Viscarret. A sign for motorists said "Camino de Santiago 775 Km.", but then that was by the surfaced highway and I expected the old route to wind a longer way to Compostela.

I was aware that nowadays considerable numbers of people travel to Santiago by coach and car and wondered how long it would take them to do so. Some might spend two or three days on the way. I expected to take four or five weeks to walk there, but then I was here for the journey.

The obvious route was along the surfaced road. It was a well-engineered carriageway through spectacular countryside and with surprisingly little traffic. There were steep passes, forests and sudden views across miles of similar terrain. As I walked I felt a burning sensation on the sole of each foot. Yesterday I had been striding purposefully up the slope to the crest of the Pyrenean ridge with the enthusiasm of the first day on the route. Too long and too quick a stride on the up-slope had caused the damage, even to feet well used to walking. Over the years I could hear myself warning others to beware of such over-keenness and like many another expert had ignored my own advice.

A car with a family party on board stopped and I was offered a lift. They moved over to make room and seemed disappointed when I declined their friendly invitation. As they drove off the children waved and shouted good wishes and their consideration took my mind off my feet. Virtually the only other traffic on the road was an occasional huge lorry laden with massive logs. These were travelling towards me in the direction of France and each driver raised an arm to greet me with the open-handed Roman salute. They would never know how much their encouragement was appreciated.

Zubiri, when I reached it, was a long, straggling village, quiet and empty at this time of the afternoon. In a café I asked about a room for the night and was directed to a restaurant at the other end of the village. I trudged back the way I had come and the young proprietor agreed that he did have a room but explained that it was beside the café at which I had first enquired. He smiled as my face fell and led the way outside to his car.

It was a tiny, comfortable room on the first floor of a building in the older part of the settlement. The balcony was just large enough to hold a chair and I sat with my bare feet airing on the wrought-iron guard rail. The blisters had arrived and I treated them with a sterilised needle and antiseptic powder.

Below me in the narrow street three children were playing and they called up, expecting me to understand. They spoke Basque or a dialect of Spanish and I was not able to make out a single word. I smiled and waved and they looked pleased to have been talking to the foreigner.

On the stroll back to the restaurant for the evening meal the village was quite different, a more familiar, friendlier place now I had somewhere to lodge and eat.

The restaurant was on the first floor and empty so I had a cold drink in the café below as I ordered a meal. When it was ready I went upstairs and the proprietor drew back the curtains which had been closed to keep out the afternoon sun. It was a large modern dining room with full-length windows on two sides over-looking the woods and the foothills. But it was still empty. The chatter drifted up from the bar and once again I had to resign myself to dining on my own in an empty room.

The spasm of loneliness lasted for a moment only and I fixed my attention on the food. The fish soup was the right starter and I began to enjoy the meal. The dessert was a glazed fruit tart, made from apples and pears and in the French style. I took the cheese and the wine downstairs for the company.

Next morning I discovered that the house in which I was lodging contained a bar on the ground floor. Like many of the shops in this area there was no sign outside or any other indication of the purpose of the establishment. Inside I sat at the high counter with racks of drinks behind and drank milky coffee from a large delph cup without handles. It was like the bowl I remembered my father using at home in Belfast for his early-morning egg-nog of weak tea, sugar and eggs.

The distance on the road passed quickly although the blisters nipped for a few moments each time I started. It was disappointing to find that I was mainly following the surfaced road and I hoped that on the other side of Pamplona the old route and the modern carriage-way would follow different lines.

It was possible to see the city from a long way off. A sweeping boulevard with a wide tree-shaded pavement climbed steeply towards the centre. The traffic noise and the fumes made it difficult to appreciate what must have been a magnificent approach to a city. I made the most of the shade and hoped that by arriving early it would be easy to find somewhere to stay. This proved not to be the case and, as I trudged around for an hour and a half, a short day's walk seemed to be changing into a long one.

The city was large and confusing and my wanderings without purpose. Eventually I found a room over a first floor restaurant and all annoyance vanished at dinner.

The dining room was on the floor below my bed-room and when I sat down at a table I was not surprised to be the only diner. It now seemed to be a predestined part of the journey. The family of the proprietor came in to the room to ask if they might use the television. They watched their favourite programmes and I enjoyed their company.

Later I found Pamplona a different city to the one I had arrived in some hours before. Every street in the old part was filled with happy strolling people. Friendly crowds of young and old gently surged through the narrow passageways. The bars and cafés were doing good business but the people were in the streets enjoying themselves without having to spend money.

There was no sign of foreigners. If present, they were, like myself, a part of the throng. It was a most cheering feeling to be sharing the life of this ancient city with its people. Then I remembered the distance I had to cover the next day and found a café where I could watch and rest in the sitting position and sip a Pyrenean liqueur. The citizens of Pamplona had made room for yet another traveller on the Road to Santiago.

CHAPTER 3

A Journey Back Through Time

Pamplona was bright and clean next morning, busy and businesslike in the sunshine. The people in the streets looked more relaxed and carefree than city-dwellers usually have a right to do. I stepped gingerly on the blisters on the sole of each foot treading as lightly as possible. By the time I reached the outskirts the blisters had decided that painful protest was hardly worth the effort and I was left with only a slight burning sensation to remind me of the folly of a previous day.

Studying the maps before I left home I had been aware that, for the first few days, a good deal of the old route was now the line of the modern road. The stretch over the Pyrenees had been an exception but since then I had mainly been following surfaced roads keeping to the pavement or verge if there was one, or walking on the very edge of the carriageway. It was some encouragement to be able to hope that the further I went the more of the Camino would be along country lanes and mountain tracks.

The only way out of Pamplona was along the motor road, narrow and dangerous to start with, leading to a pleasant section on a country road before coming back to the main highway for the steep climb to the pass. It was 700m of ascent and in the heat and the traffic fumes it felt higher. I passed an ancient well at the roadside but there was a notice saying that the water was not for drinking. As the road reached the crest the new carriageway had been cut deeply into the ridge.

It was time for lunch so I climbed above the road and found the remnants of the old route winding through the trees and across the range at the original pass. This was the Alto del Perdon. The view was superb, across scrub land and sierra, looking back towards Pamplona and, in front of me, stretching over the valley of the Rio Agra in the direction of Puente la Reina, the way I was bound.

The ancient track was completely deserted. Below I could hear the traffic in the cutting as a dull roar. There was a light breeze which made the Alto a fresh and airy place. As I emptied my rucksac to prepare for lunch the loneliness returned but only briefly as if I needed to be reminded at these moments that I was still on my own.

There was great pleasure in stretching full length on a bed of pine needles under the trees and waiting for the water to boil for brewing tea. I ate and rested at leisure and felt the benefit of the break more than on previous days.

It was reassuring to have the few items of equipment that I had brought with me and I packed them with care. For those used to carrying a rucksac the frameless type is best. It requires some skill in the packing but is more comfortable and less effort to carry. The packing should shape the sac to the back with the heaviest items being placed high and close to the shoulder blades. The light-weight sleeping bag went in first to shape the bottom of the sac. The change of clothes was next, and useful padding against the back, shorts, spare shirt, socks, underpants and light training shoes. There was still plenty of room for the small toilet kit of tooth brush and razor, a tiny towel and the water-proof anorak. The heavier items, two cameras, an aluminium dixie containing most of the spare food, a small gaz stove and the two water-bottles were packed near the top and held in place by the softer items.

Into the outside pockets went the mug, spoon, knife, notebooks, pens, first aid kit, spare films and the rest of the food. The sac was comfortably full and felt reasonably light. I swung it on to my back and it fitted as if it had been ergonomically designed for the job.

The long slope wound slowly down and near Puente I reached the place where the pilgrim routes from France traditionally came together. From three of the starting points, Paris, Vézelay and Le Puy, the ways joined near St. Jean Pied-de-Port and crossed the Pyrenees by the pass which I had used. The most southerly of the starting places was Arles and this route crossed the Pyrenees further west at the Col du Somport, to meet up with the other ways at this point.   A new motor road sweeps around Puente la Reina to cross the river Agra and I left the wide carriageway to enter the town by a narrow street. It was obvious why the vehicles had to be diverted around the town. This was a settlement dating from times when there was advantage in having narrow passageways and now these protected it from the modern menace of through traffic.

Such was the immediate spell of Puente that for the first time I felt truly on the Camino Francés. In spite of the mountain track in the Pyrenees too much of the route had been in the company of vehicles. The past had only revealed itself in glimpses, brief sightings of an ancient building or landmark. Now it was different. The feel of the Pilgrimage was in Puente. From here on it would be easy to make the link with the past.

It was a strange exciting feeling to have made contact so quickly and so directly. This was no gentle process of increasing awareness of an empathy with the pilgrims of ancient times. It was a dramatic leap backwards to land on the old route.

stones laid in a pattern which made a central spine to give height in the middle of the track. This would cause the rain water to run off at either side without eroding the surface by allowing it to become a watercourse.

I met a friendly shepherd with a great flock of healthy looking sheep and rose to higher ground with a view over a huge tract of countryside. Looking back the line of the route curved and twisted, fitting the slope of the land, trailing out behind as far as the eye could see, an almost white line etched into the landscape.

The Rio Salado looked an agreeable river when I reached it and a story came to mind as told by Amery Picaud in the Codex Calixtinus. He described a party of pilgrims arriving at the banks of the river in the twelfth century. Two local men were seated on the near bank sharpening their knives and the pilgrims asked if the water was safe to drink. The locals' reply in the affirmative did not fully convince the travellers so they let their animals drink first. Two beasts died immediately and the local men stepped forward to claim the carcasses. By trade they were mule skinners.

When he passed this way forty years ago, and knowing of the story in the Codex, Walter Starkie tasted the water of the Salado. He found it brackish but suffered no dire consequences. I decided that I was not thirsty.

The day became increasingly hot and when it came time for a break at mid-day there was no where to sit in the shade. Even the breeze was warm. In desperation I pushed my way into a hedge at the side of a field. The sun was overhead and it was necessary to get right into the thicket to try to shelter from the burning rays. The upper branches were only sparsely leafed and I crouched and sweated, retreating deeper without relief, trying to eat and drink a little and rest my legs and feet.

I thought of the idyllic spot for lunch on the previous day on the Col de Perdon and it helped. But it was a losing battle and I gave up without feeling that I had properly fed, watered and rested. It always seems easy to do without food in the heat of the middle of the day but a long journey requires sufficient food as fuel for energy. Late evening is a pleasant time for the main meal of the day but for most people it is not the ideal time to take in a large quantity of nourishment. Over a few days it would hardly matter but I was conscious that on a long journey it is easy to use up the reserves and so reduce the physical capacity to keep going.

Once I was on the way again the blisters throbbed for a few moments and then gave up the attempt to add to the difficulties. Half an hour later the problems of the day might never have existed. I was swinging along as if now acclimatised to the heat and enjoying the route as I had done earlier.

The town of Estella appeared on a height on the north side of the road. A few kilometres earlier an alternative branch of the Camino would have allowed a short-cut across the valley of the Rio Ega but Estella was too important and, by all accounts, too attractive a stopping place to be missed.

Even the Codex Calixtinus had been complimentary. Its editor, Amery Picaud, had been exceedingly critical of the Basque region through which I had just passed and particularly so of its people. He had, however, taken the trouble to set down a list of Basque words and their meanings, probably the first written text in that language. Amery must have reached Estella with great relief. In this town the medieval pilgrims found good food, wine and accommodation. The inhabitants made them truly welcome. The minstrels travelling with the pilgrims sang the praises of the town and called it 'Estella la Bella'.

Amery Picaud recorded that it was full of every blessing. He mentioned interesting local customs and was taken by the fine character of the people. In contrast to his anecdote about the Rio Salado just down the road, he praised the waters of the town as pleasant and healthy.

I wondered if Estella could still live up to its reputation, aware that the recommendations of others are not always borne out in practice, particularly when so many centuries have passed.

It was now four in the afternoon and when I found an inn, the hectic activity of a celebratory lunch was still keeping the staff of two fully occupied. However, the woman in charge and the girl who was serving at table had time to welcome me cheerfully. They looked flushed with effort but took to the prospect of looking after one more guest without fuss and between serving great armsful of dishes of dessert.

The inn was in the old part of the town and when I was settled in I went to the main square and sat under the colonnades to watch the life of Estella parade before me. The long, cold drink of white rum and Coca Cola cost more than twice as much as it had done the previous evening in Puente la Reina. But then in grand cities like Paris, Athens or Istanbul the cafés with the best situations always charge something for the view.

The modern part of Estella is spacious and elegant. The old and the new fit together as if designed to do so. It was no surprise to discover that the Spanish society which encourages interest in the Pilgrimage, Los Amigos del Camino de Santiago, have their headquarters in the town. Its influence and that of the French society have been significant factors in the development of interest in the ancient route. These two bodies undertake scholarly research and publish the type of current information which I had found so hard to come by before leaving. Bruno had made

The Bridge at Puente La Reina.

me aware of the existence of this material and enabled me to have a brief glance at it at Puente. I decided that, if he and I met again at Navarrete, I would study it with care and take notes.

The church in the main square was deserted in the early evening and as I sat for a few moments in one of its pews I found that the stillness of Puente had travelled with me to Estella. The wooden seat was comfortable to the point where I could sit without moving, or wondering how long I could stay there, as if the evening had paused to give me time to think.

The restaurant I chose for an evening meal had been decorated forty or fifty years ago with flair and in the flamboyant style of that time. It had a well-cared-for look but it was empty when I entered. When I left an hour later after a reasonable meal, once again I had been the only diner.

Strolling in the evening between the old and the new town I found myself enjoying the atmosphere of Estella in the same way as pilgrims must have done since Amery Picaud praised the place in his guide book all those centuries ago.

My room at the inn was cosy and restful and I slept well. I had paid the bill before going to bed and when I left in the morning there was no one about. After the function of the previous day the management and staff, all two of them, were obviously having a well-deserved lie-in.

The sky over Estella was dull and heavy with rain. The town had been worth the detour and I left behind a place with a sense of history and people with minds of their own. Picaud, and others since, who have sung the praises of Estella la Bella are still right.

Estella la Bella is not to be missed.

The rain began before I was clear of the outskirts. It was a steady, gentle drizzle, like the damp of a soft Irish day, but warmer, much warmer. I hung my water-proof anorak over my shoulders covering the rucksac and the upper part of the body but open at the front. Walking steadily, the first twenty kilometres seemed to pass quickly.

I passed through Los Arcos which looked interesting, even in the rain, and followed the old route on a track running parallel to the road for ten kilometres. Back on the main road near Torres del Rio a young man passed me in a car sounding his horn and waving. He made a U-turn and drove back to talk to me. He was in his early twenties, lean and athletic and talked excitedly, the words tumbling out, one on top of the other. It was difficult to make any sense of what he was saying in such high-speed Spanish.

Eventually I gathered that he had walked to Santiago the previous year and wanted to take me to his home so that his mother could cook me a meal. We arranged to meet at the next cross-roads in ten minutes and he sped off home to say that they would soon be having a guest. I waited at the cross-roads in the shelter of a large tree but there was no sign of the young man. After three-quarters of an hour I decided that I must have misunderstood and walked on towards Torres knowing that he could catch up on me if he had been delayed.

The rest had done me good and, when I reached Torres and found that there was no inn, the prospect of another ten kilometres to Viana, after the thirty odd kilometres so far, was not in the least daunting. I had missed a meal and a chance to meet a local family but the waiting had given me a much-needed and refreshing break.

Two hours later I saw Viana perched on a hill above a huge retaining and defensive wall built of cut stone. A woman answered the door of a little house below the wall and pointed upwards when I asked about the inn. I trudged up the long slope on a road which curved around the wall and came out at the town on the top of the hill.

The rain had eased but the sky was still dark grey and, in the poor light the stone buildings and damp streets gave the town a severe and forbidding aspect. There were other elements too, which gave this town an atmosphere completely different from any other I had experienced so far. My instincts for survival detected an air of malevolence and a hint of menace as soon as my feet reached the pavements of this damp, grey town.

A festival had been in progress since early morning and its debris littered the streets, empty wine bottles, cartons, wrapping paper, torn banners and streamers and damp, discarded leaflets stuck to the pavements. The bars were still full of singing, roaring, carousing men, sticking it out to the bitter end.

I asked for directions and was eventually taken by the only sober-looking man I could find and led down a side street to a bar. I thanked my guide and he left at speed when he saw the mob inside. The room was awash with spilled wine, broken glasses and men in various stages of inebriation. Some were happily drunk, others uproariously so but those who had reached the belligerent stage were making their presence felt.

The land-lord and his wife were behind the bar. They were both large and looked as tough as this job requires but they were worried. Their customers were out of control and it was obvious that the serious trouble could start at any moment.

The land-lord nodded when I pushed my way to the bar and asked if this was the inn.

"¿Por favor, teine usted una habitación para mí?" If ever I needed the right words to ask for a room I needed them now and this sentence had worked when I had asked for a room on the previous evenings.

He understood first time and turned to consult his wife. She shook her head in a way that brooked no argument and harangued him at the very idea of it. I imagined that she was telling him in no uncertain terms that he had enough on his hands without taking in some stray traveller to stay the night.

He turned back to me and shook his head slowly. "Cerrado" he said and I knew he meant that he would be closed once he had cleared the bar. He looked at me sadly as if he was sorry that he was not able to offer a room at the inn.

I left him to his own troubles and outside the drizzle had turned to rain. Water dripped and ran in little gutters from the colonnades. The poor light was fading as night closed in, much earlier than usual. There was nothing for it but to try elsewhere in the town.

CHAPTER 5

Chaos and Order

The buildings of Viana were solid, heavily-made constructions, and might have been designed as part of the fortifications of the town. Narrow streets ran off a central plaza with a fountain still spouting in the rain. It looked as though this place had changed little over the past few hundred years. There must have been dark, damp evenings here for the pilgrims of old. It occurred to me that the scene in the bar had probably been enacted many times in the past and the likelihood was that pilgrims would have been amongst the carousers.

Unlike the lively scene in Estella the previous evening, when spruce policemen in bright red Basque berets joked and laughed with the strollers, there was no sign of any representatives of law and order in Viana. Local people who were not still involved in the revels were keeping clear of this part of the town. The hint of menace which I had felt on the way into the town was stronger now. For anyone expecting to find moments of fear along the Road to Santiago, this place might have seemed dangerous.

As I walked down a narrow street towards the plaza six young men approached from the opposite direction, in line abreast. Their arms were linked and they stretched across the full width of the passageway. The youngest would have been about nineteen and four of the others in their early twenties. One was older, he was the noisiest, a balding, paunchy man in his thirties. All six were drunk, rowdily, loudly drunk. Shouting and chanting, they pulled each other from side to side as they staggered along laughing at the joke of it.

They saw me coming and focussed their attention on the foreigner. I grinned at them, probably an ugly grin that showed the teeth in the way that some animals do in such circumstances, and kept straight on. When we met they formed a circle around me jigging and dancing, slapping me on the back, shouting in my ear. I raised an arm to free myself. They gave way and I pressed on, waving to them over my shoulder.

I found a second inn eventually and the door was closed. Having knocked, for what seemed like the tenth time without response, a man came from across the road to tell me he thought the inn would be open in half an hour.

Back in the plaza a water fight was in progress. A supply of plastic bags had been discovered. Boys and men were filling them at the fountain pool and hurling them at each other and any passer-by foolish enough to venture into their arena. It might have been wiser to keep to the pavement under the colonnades but the shortest way was across the plaza close to the fountain. In my tired state there was no possibility of compromise. It was the obvious route and I took it.

The six I had met in the side street were in the thick of the action and, while water bombs were exploding all around, my passage seemed protected. The six shouted something incomprehensible. It sounded like encouragement. Were they acting as my guardian angels?

I was guided to another inn but it proved to be the one I had visited first approached from a different direction. The land-lord was still trying to remove his patrons and they were objecting to such ungrateful treatment by knocking the furniture about and breaking glasses and bottles.

With no police to turn to, the situation in the bar, like the rest of the centre of the town, seemed out of control. I wondered how they managed to keep order on such an evening in medieval times, at the end of a day of festival awash with wine.

I sat down on a stone step, in the shelter of a doorway in a side street, badly in need of a rest, trying to look inconspicuous. The revels and the ructions flowed and ebbed around me. There were moments of calm which would suddenly become ominous as the next group of carousers appeared around a corner. Sitting where I was on the step, they ignored me and I turned up my toes to ease the painful soles and the stiffness in the backs of my legs.

The shops were shut and shuttered and I felt in my rucksac for the last of the food. It came easily to hand, an apple and four biscuits. They tasted good and I drank the last of the water. I had a feeling that there must be something symbolic about this particular moment but, just now, its significance eluded me.

The street lights emphasised the solidity, the permanence and the age of my surroundings and the hour passed quickly. I rose and turned back to the plaza on the way to see if the second inn was now open.

The water fight was almost over. Three or four boys were trying to keep it going. The six young men were still there and the boys were wisely throwing the water bombs only at each other. The youngest and the oldest of the six were sitting on the rim of the fountain, heads in their hands, looking, and no doubt feeling, exceedingly sorry for themselves. Two of the others were squabbling, shouting and pushing at each other, trying to fight.

The remaining two saw me coming and linked arms with me as if with an old friend. They offered what appeared to be their last bottle of wine and I took a great swig out of courtesy and on the principle that my need was greater than theirs.

The wine caught me in the back of the throat as sharp as a ripe lime. This was no smooth, well-rounded red, produced with tender care for delicate palates. It was raw and fresh. It left the mouth clean and warmed the stomach. But it was not a wine for drinking in sips and I reached for the bottle and tried again. It tasted even better. I could think of old friends of mine who would regard this as the ideal drinking wine. My two new friends were delighted that I was enjoying it and offered me the bottle again. Had they been less intoxicated I might have asked them to find me accommodation, but the evening was slipping away and the odds were long against them being able to do so.

When I arrived back at the second inn it was still closed and shuttered. As I was knocking a woman opened the door of a house nearby and told me that the land-lord would not be back until the next day.

It was time to decide whether to continue to look for a room here or face the walk to Logrono. It was an easy choice. Viana seemed to have closed its doors to me and, although I had already covered almost forty kilometres and had been tramping around the town for what seemed like hours, it would be only another two hours steady walking. It was no time to be afraid of a few kilometres.

The long sweep from the town to the main road below the retaining wall was a good time to tell myself that the legs were not as tired as they felt. Going well, I would be in Logrono at ten-thirty, by Spanish standards not too late to find a room and a meal.

Once the effort was made to make a start the depression began to lift. Strangely it seemed important that I would come back to this town some other time to see another of its faces.

This visit had been on a wet, dismal evening when the fun and joy of a fiesta were fizzling out like a damp fire-work. The menace had not materialised and no one had shown me ill-will. The failure to find a room and a meal was my own and largely due to my lack of facility in the Spanish language. By the time I had reached the road I had made my peace with Viana and resolved to return.

The light was fading quickly and the main road was narrow and unlit. There was no footpath on either side or even a verge to walk on. The surface was bordered by a rough bank overgrown with bushes. I walked on the left side to face the traffic and each time a car or lorry approached I had to step up on to the bank in case the driver failed to see me. As a pedestrian at night, it is easy to think that because the walker can see the vehicle, its driver will see the walker. It pays not to depend that this will be the case. I remembered Bruno's story of being struck by a lorry crossing the Pyrenean pass and being taken to hospital.

A few kilometres further on an old car, with the bonnet and one door a different colour to the rest of the bodywork, pulled over beside me and stopped. The driver was a man in his early twenties and the other occupants were a girl of about the same age who looked like his sister and an older man who might have been their father. They were going the same way as I was and offered me a lift.

I accepted too quickly. They too had been to the festival in Viana and were all drunk. Almost as soon as we started the car ran out of petrol and the driver let it coast through a gap in the bank into a field. They left the car with me still sitting in it and, laughing and shouting, made their way towards a small dilapidated house set back from the road.

It was obviously their little joke to offer me a lift when they had almost reached the end of their journey. I smiled ruefully and made my way back to the road. For anyone inclined to take themselves too seriously this would have been a time to feel angry. However, it was but a small insult to the dignity. Being made to look foolish was much to be preferred to being given a lift by these revellers.

Nearer Logrono the volume of traffic increased. The banks at the side of the road had gone and in their place was a verge overgrown with spikey bushes. When a vehicle approached it was necessary to push myself in amongst these. When the cars and lorries came in convoy I had to stop, waiting in the jungle until the last one had passed.

For once there was a comparative lull and a car travelling in my direction on the other side of the road stopped. The driver wound down his window and offered me a lift. It was only two kilometres to Logrono and in spite of the previous experience I accepted immediately.

A betting man would know that the odds were not yet in my favour but this time the gamble came off. We reached the city in minutes with my benefactor driving smoothly and well. He spoke a little English and warned against walking the roads at night.

"Sometimes the drivers drink alcohol." he said slowly and sternly, by way of warning and I agreed, with feeling. He stopped in a main thoroughfare in Logrono and pointed down a side street.

"Good hotel." he said "Not expensive." We shook hands and he wished me well on the journey. "Stay a few days in Logrono" he shouted after me "You will like it". The evening was beginning to look up.

In twenty minutes I had been shown to my room, was unpacked, showered, changed and on the way to the main plaza to look for somewhere to eat. Viana seemed so far away that I was beginning to wonder if my visit there had not been a dark day-dream on a wet evening's walk in strange countryside.

Logrono was a city in relaxed, happy mood, busily functioning at the peak of its evening life. I found a bar with a corner curtained off to form a small dining area. The bar itself was panelled in dark wood and cleverly lit by old lamps with coloured glass shades. The curtain separating the dining area was red and heavy and hung in deep folds from a substantial brass rod. It was a comfortable, welcoming place, the bar buzzing with conversation and the dining alcove calm and restful.

Once past Viana I had left the Province of Navarre and gone beyond the eastern extremity of the Basque country. I was now in the north-western corner of the ancient region of Castile and Leon. This is the Province of La Rioja, famous for its food and wine.

I asked for a local dish and the woman in charge brought me a steaming earthenware casserole.

"¿Cómo se llama?" I said trying to show a little confidence and hoping that this meant "What is it called?".

"Cocido." she said lifting the lid and smiling. "Nostro cocido." It was just the dish for me at the end of such a day. Cocido is a traditional chick-pea hotpot with a great variety of regional variations and I was about to try this bar's own version.The recipe is usually based on chicken, beef, ham and garlic sausage and they were all present.

Surprisingly there was a wine list and it was long, with a range of prices not usual in such a small establishment. This, of course, is the land of the finest Spanish wine, Rioja, and the list had to be appropriately representative. The house wine, the vino de casa, was itself a Rioja and some way from being the cheapest on the list. It was certain to be a contrast to the wine of Viana which I had shared with the revellers. The first sip told me that I had managed to choose well again.

The cocido arrived at the table still bubbling away in its crock and as it cooled I sampled the wine. It was a shade of deep red, sparkling in the low light. It was smooth on the tongue, much more so than any other I had tasted so far on the journey. It was not a wine for sipping and discussing nor for gulping without ceremony. It was simply a wine for enjoying.

In the Codex Calixtinus, Amery Picaud recommended the wines of Rioja as being excellent and, as the writer was French and rarely lavish with his praise, it was commendation indeed. It seems entirely fitting that the wines of this region are still regarded by experts as being amongst the best in the world.

The meal was appetising and substantial and I did it justice. I mopped up the last of the cocido and the sauce with slices of bread cut from a round loaf. The senora approved when she saw the dish empty and wiped clean. She offered another helping but I had to thank her and decline.

She served a goat cheese with a sharp distinctive taste. Cheese and wine is the simplest way to end a meal and here, nothing could have been more fitting.

I left the bar and wandered through colonnaded streets in the old part of the city. The crowds were smaller than Pamplona, just as friendly but more reservedly so. In a small, packed café I ordered an anisette liqueur and the customers moved up to make room for me on a wooden bench. I sat with my legs stretched. The aches eased to the point where it felt like the tiredness of a single day on the mountain rather than the burning weariness of the last stretch.

On the way back to the hotel I decided to have the morning off as a half day's rest. It was only ten or twelve kilometres to Navarrete where I hoped to meet Bruno again. I reckoned that I had covered about one hundred and eighty kilometres in six days. A little time off in Logrono seemed a very attractive and sensible idea.

Stretched out full length on a comfortable bed, I thought again of my visit to Viana and tried to assure myself that it had really happened.

It was such a short distance and time away but seemed much further back in my mind. If it had not been a dark day-dream perhaps it had all happened in some previous life.

I smiled in the darkness looking up towards the ceiling I could not see and was asleep before I could turn over.

My dreams were of boisterous revels in a medieval town not unlike Viana; and of joining the locals in the merry-making.

During the night I awoke with a great thirst and drank over half a litre of water. A long walk, even on a wet day, can leave the body dehydrated and drinking wine should always be complemented by drinking water. With my thirst slaked I felt content, relaxed and sleepy again. Back in bed I turned on my side and slept until late.

At least eight-thirty seemed late until I realised that I had a half day's rest in front of me. An hour later the day was already warm and the great square of Logrono was spacious and clean with its central area set out like a small park.

Needing to replenish my cash reserves I found a bank and was directed to the third floor to change a Eurocheque. Once on that floor I wandered around for a few minutes looking, without success, for a sign and was shown into a large office with a well-dressed man sitting behind a grandly imposing desk.

When I made my request in halting Spanish he looked at me pleasantly and spoke in English.

"I rarely have the opportunity to use your language. Do you mind if we speak English?". He had learned to speak the language at college in England and spoke carefully with obvious enjoyment.

As he filled in the forms we talked and when he heard that I was on the pilgrim route he asked me how I was travelling. I answered that I was walking, trying not to sound as if I was expecting praise for so doing. Up to this point the bank official had been interested and courteous, now he became concerned and involved.

"Some day I will go to Santiago." he said "I have made a promise." He looked serious and we let the conversation pause while he contemplated the idea of his own pilgrimage.

"Let me give you a little hospitality." he said at length "A cup of coffee to help a peregrino on his way."

He locked his room, obtained the cash for me from the cashier on the ground floor and led the way out into the square. We strolled to an elegant café, built half-underground, fronted by a patio with trees and shrubs. It was busy with smart morning customers and as we sipped café solo he plied me with questions about the route.

"When I go to Santiago," he said "It will be only a car trip." He looked apologetic. "It is a poor way to make such a pilgrimage."

It seemed sad that my journey might undermine his feelings for his, so I changed the subject and cheered him up with my tale of old Viana.

On the way back he took me to the tourist office for the official booklet on the Road to Santiago. Although they had copies in Spanish, French and German, to his great disappointment they had none in English. I took the French edition, not having the heart to tell him that I had the English version back at the hotel.

"It is for those who travel by car," he said.

The booklet is indeed designed with the car traveller in mind but it is a beautifully produced and illustrated outline of the pilgrimage and its route. It contains historical background and notes about each section of the journey. Where the traditional way and the motor road diverge, the booklet details the best route for those travelling by car or coach.

Before we parted, the bank official - I suspected that he might be the manager by the size of his office and the way he had been treated by the other staff - printed his name and telephone number in my note-book.

"This is in case you need help." he said "If you are in difficulty on the road to Santiago, if something is wrong, telephone me and I will come to you wherever you are". It was a generous offer to be made to a complete stranger but the further I travelled along the Camino Francés the easier it was for me to understand such a gesture.

Logrono is a modern city which has managed to preserve much of its past. Once it was known as 'the city of the steeples' and Walter Starkie felt that the spire of the 14th century St. Maria del Palacio was, without doubt, the most beautiful in Spain. He was impressed too by the statue of Santiago Matamoros - St. James, slayer of the Moors - and understandably so, for it is an immense and powerful image. He saw the Saint as strikingly defiant and the horse as the only one along the Camino worthy of carrying St. James.

The cathedral was empty, a cool retreat from the mid-morning heat. Sitting quietly in a place like this, a mystical awareness of the pilgrimage was gradually being revealed to me. Meeting Bruno had given me a contact with the religious fervour and sincerity of the pilgrims. Here, in this calm interior, it was possible to feel their presence by their passage over the years.

I wondered about the real reasons, perhaps the hidden reasons for my own journey. To follow the cult of St. James to Santiago requires a sense of religious purpose based on a sincere belief in its truth, a belief which I did not have. I was on the Camino for the journey, to follow the footsteps of those who had gone before. From the beginning, and much to my surprise, I had been accepted as a true Santiago pilgrim. Now I was beginning to understand what that entailed but had a sense of being a pilgrim in another way. It was outside the dogma of the cult but still meant living and travelling as they did.

As I sat on the hard pew, single worshippers entered, prayed and left so quietly that it was possible to sense their presence without hearing their movements. Their faith was a simple, natural act and I could feel the strength of it.

Out in the street the morning was over. Shop and office workers streamed out of the buildings on their mid-day break. They were in a hurry, crowding the pavements, talking and laughing with all the enjoyment of those temporarily released from close confinement.

It took ten minutes or more to find a café which was not too full and which offered a good selection of tapas, those tempting, savoury snacks designed to keep the Spanish going between proper meals. At the counter I selected split, hard boiled eggs dressed with anchovies, a fresh sardine crisply fried and a slice of tortilla. Tortilla, the potato omelette, is one of the most common and sustaining of tapas. It is usually served cold and cost here, in the city centre, only a few pesetas.

I put off the journey to Navarrete for a few hours longer. It was only a few kilometres and it would be cooler later in the afternoon. The longer I spent here resting, the more opportunity there was for my foot to heal. These were reasons enough and, after the continuous physical activity of the past week, it was easy to slip into a pleasant state of relaxation.

I sat on a shaded seat in the main plaza and watched the afternoon life of Logrono take its course. At about three o'clock I roused myself from the luxury of the siesta and decided that it was time to be on the way. I collected my rucksac from the hotel and felt that the day was hotter than ever. But there were no doubts. The rest had made me feel refreshed and the sense of purpose was strong, even stronger than it had been when I started.

It was as if I now knew which pilgrim route I was travelling.

CHAPTER 6

Bruno: The Real Pilgrim

One side of the street was shaded on the way out of Logrono and I made the most of it. The city thoroughfares gave way eventually to the open road and I came out into the full heat and glare of the sun. However, difficulties do not always compound themselves and by then the pain of the blisters had receded to a dull ache. The road began to climb steadily on a long, upward curve. The hill seemed very steep and long but that may well have been an impression created by the hot slog at this stage of the day.

I crested a rise, a false brow of the hill, and saw a figure ahead. Like me, the walker was facing the traffic, keeping well into the left hand side of the road. The distance between us reduced and I could see that it was a man, striding along with a slightly limping gait. He wore boots and breeches. From his rucksac protruded a long wand with a white pennant at its tip, waving and bobbing, pointing to the sky. It could only be Bruno. Bruno the real pilgrim.

For a few strides I stepped up the pace, eager to catch him before he reached the top of the hill. Then I remembered, that in Puente la Reina, we had agreed to walk alone and to meet at dinner and breakfast if we were staying at the same inn. I dropped back and let the slight figure lead me at that distance.

In a few moments I was aware that there was a second figure, smaller and more lightly made than Bruno, dressed in brown, keeping to the rough ground to his left. I took off my sun-glasses to see if the lenses had been playing tricks with my sight and the two figures were even clearer. They bobbed along almost touching, then moved a metre or so apart as the smaller figure seemed to skip over the rough ground, picking the best route. Bruno tramped along like me, on the very inside edge of the surfaced carriageway, setting the pace for his companion.

On the road bridge overlooking Navarrete I stopped to catch a cool air and to rest my aching feet. By the time I reached the village Bruno and his companion were nowhere to be seen. I took a room at the inn he had recommended and celebrated my arrival, as always, and in spite of the shortness of the route, with a cool drink.

liked was a simple consequence of being away from home? They flitted across the plaza bounded by the Parador and the cathedral, as complete a contrast to Bruno and his fellow pilgrims as the mind could imagine.

The Parador looked as if it might have been in place as long as the cathedral. Bruno had warned me against staying at such places.

"A pilgrim's needs are simple." I could hear him say, "Paradores are too grand for us. We must have a clean place to eat and sleep and nothing to keep us from the road."

In spite of the warning and having lodged in comfort at Paradores on previous visits to Spain, I went to have a look around.

Successive Spanish Governments have a great deal to be proud of in the development of their nation-wide chain of hotels called Paradores National. Many are converted castles or other notable ancient buildings, others are new structures designed and constructed to fit the architectural traditions of their locality. All are finished and furnished with taste and style. Although one is regarded amongst the very best hotels in Europe and priced accordingly, the majority are for the ordinary tourist and traveller and are first rate value.

Here is a rest house originally provided by Domingo beside his church, repaired in the 14th century and now re-built and converted as a Parador National. Inside it is beautifully restored and its patrons are tourists or pilgrims travelling by car or luxury coach, still an important resting place on the Road to Santiago.

In the foyer an American couple were trying to make a telephone call and using what is sometimes called the English method of communicating with foreigners. If they don't understand, speak louder. If they still don't understand, shout!

The male receptionist was trying to be helpful in the most courteous way. He spoke English quite well but was beginning to wilt under the barrage of sustained rudeness. It emerged that the number they were trying to contact in America was engaged but somehow that failed to exonerate the receptionist, the hotel, the Spanish telephone system and Spain in general.

It was the first time in nearly two weeks that I had heard any version of the English language spoken by someone for whom it was their native tongue and it was a shock. No harm to the Parador, it looked like a beautiful place to stay, but I was glad I was booked in at the hostal with the nuns and the old folk and Bruno the proper pilgrim.

Across the plaza the cathedral was cool and silent and, at that moment, empty of people. I sat down in a front pew aware that this place had been here, much as it was now, for the past eight hundred years. For the first time since I left St. Jean Pied-de-Port I was conscious that the Road was effecting a change in me. There was a feeling of calmness, an absence of tension and, in spite of tiredness, a sense of physical relaxation. In this particular way and to this degree, these were new sensations.

All around were the manifestations of faith. The passage of hundreds of thousands of believers over hundreds of years had created its own atmosphere. That I was able to sense it so strongly was a surprise. My own belief acknowledged the existence of a supreme being and here that felt confirmed. I was no closer to accepting that God might be contracted to one specific religion or sect, the followers of which would have exclusive rights to his services. That seemed such a basely human thought that, in the context of how God might act, it was to me completely unbelievable. Yet without the strength, organisation and support of such a religion all this indication of His presence around me would have perished.

In the shrines of other religions in London, Istanbul, New Delhi and Ladakh on the borders of Tibet, the same feeling had been with me. Had the very separateness of the faiths of the Catholic, Protestant, Jew, Moslem, Buddhist, Hindu and all aided the continuation of their beliefs?

I sat in the tranquillity of the half light and wondered what God wanted me to do. There was too, a feeling of relief at being able to ask the question.

My mind turned from the present to the past and to the famous pilgrim story of the cock and hen. It was one of those tales attached firmly to the pilgrimage, originally passed on by word of mouth and now an important part of pilgrim lore. It had been a surprise to find that so many writers on the pilgrimage had taken it seriously and I had decided not to gawp as others obviously did at the cage in the cathedral which still houses a cock and a hen.

That was more easily said than done. The cage for the fowl was huge, placed high on a wall near the door and as I left, with my eyes well used to the dim light, it could not be ignored. It was carved in wood, barred, ornate, and with a live cock and hen in residence strutting noisily from side to side. This gothic masterpiece must be the most splendid chicken coop in the world.

The story recounts that a young pilgrim was wrongly accused of stealing, summarily tried, sentenced and hanged on the same day. That evening at dinner, the judge was saying that the young man was as surely guilty, as the cock he was about to carve was roasted, when the cock rose on the carving tray and crowed. Servants sent to the prison for the young man's body, found him alive and well and all was forgiven. One version of the story has it that the young man had repulsed the advances of a local girl and that she had hidden a stolen silver goblet in his belongings before informing on him.

As I watched the cock and the hen strut proudly to and fro as if aware of the privilege of their accommodation, it seemed arrogant to regard the fascination with this story as merely the faith of the gullible. We all have need of our myths.

It was too dark for a photograph without flash but I decided to take one anyway. As I set the camera for minimum light the door of the cathedral opened and a Spanish family entered. There were at least three discernable generations, children, parents and grandparents. They were on an outing and excited to be in a place of such religious importance. They clustered around the wall below the cage, pointing, exclaiming, both parents telling the story to the children at the same time. They began to look for feathers as pilgrims have done for centuries, the children crawling in the corners and the grandfather waving his hat at the birds in the hope that they would flutter their wings and shed a few.

It was omen enough. The silent, mystical calm had gone but the joy of these people in their faith was simple proof of the power of belief.

Outside the day was still almost at full heat. The plaza was busy and I had a feeling that Domingo would have been pleased with the visit of the family to his church and with the way his town had grown.

My wandering had left me late for dinner at the hostal. Bruno was already busily engaged on the soup course and he rose to shake hands.

"You like the Hostal Santa Teresita?" he asked, beaming with pride and requiring no answer.

"I say to the sisters you are coming. The Parador is not like this. I say to the sisters that you have no pass. You will pay less because I say to them you are a peregrino."

It was pleasant to hear Bruno rattle on and tell me again that I was a pilgrim. I explained the doubt in my mind that I was a genuine Santiago pilgrim but he raised his hand, like the policeman he once had been, to stop me.

"You walk like a peregrino." he said. Perhaps he meant that I was taking the journey day by day, happy to be on the pilgrim road. I wondered what he would have made of my thoughts in the cathedral. He jerked me back into the conversation.

"Yesterday I have met an old peregrino. He has been on the camino for many months. He is from Austria. He has an injury of his heart but is not ill now. Each day he walks only ten or fifteen kilometres. He has much information on the camino. It is his life study."

By now I was used to Bruno's way of speaking English. The short sentences tumbled out one after the other. He repeated words and phrases, searching for the right meaning, speaking with that total lack of self-consciousness which is an essential part of communicating effectively in someone else's language.

The old pilgrim had solved the problem of the lack of inns at frequent enough intervals by asking the priest, at each village at which he stayed, to ring ahead to the priest at the next suitable village to request that accommodation be arranged.

I knew from earlier conversations that Bruno was concerned about the length and difficulties of that part of the route from Astorga across the mountains to Pontferrada. Sure enough he had talked to the old pilgrim about this section.

"The old peregrino says that the dogs are bad in the lower villages. In the mountains the villages are deserted and he says there are wolves." He looked at me, wondering if I would laugh at the idea of wolves in the mountains of Spain.

"Is it true?" he asked so seriously that I felt I had to reassure him.

He listened intently, asking questions to make sure he understood, as I told him tales of seeing wolf tracks in the mountains of Turkey, of watching two scrawny wolves cross a scree slope in Iran and of the bear who lived behind a rock buttress, half a mile from our base camp high in the Elburz mountains of that same country.

The Road to Santiago runs across the width of Spain through the foothills of the Cantabrian mountains and over outrider ranges of this chain. The area of Bruno's concern lay far to the west, many days walk away. There the route crosses the Montes de Leon before winding over the Cantabrians themselves as the main ridge turns south and forms the barrier to the Province of Galicia.

I said that I thought that the last of the wolves had been killed in these ranges in the early part of this century at the same time as the last of the bears. It occurred to me that the old pilgrim's 'wolves' might be in reality wild dogs. When I mentioned this Bruno nodded and then, with the great seriousness with which he always gave me advice about the pilgrimage, he said

"For the mountains we must find a pilgrim's . . .". He hesitated, searching for the right word. He tried "plank" and, when that brought no reassuring look from me, said "log".

I was embarrassed at being so slow on the uptake.

"Staff" I said "We need a pilgrim staff" I stood up and gripped an imaginary staff at chest height. Bruno laughed and continued with his advice.

"It must be two metres long. The village of Foncebadon is the most dangerous place. The old pilgrim says that we must not follow the old way through the village. It is better to walk around, away from the houses."

There is an alternative route for this section following the motor road over the Manzanal Pass. I was aware that, unlike myself, Bruno often preferred the surfaced road to the lanes and mountain tracks. However the Austrian had told him that the mountain route was the proper one for pilgrims and he was determined to follow it.

From the time that I had begun to plan the journey I had regarded this as one of the most interesting parts of the entire Camino. It was obviously too, one of the most challenging sections and I wondered how the old pilgrim would fare. Bruno, of course, had asked him and had learned that the Austrian hoped to stay in the lower villages on either side of the pass and have company for the higher section of the route.

"You and I, we like to walk alone," said Bruno "But if we come to Astorga on the same day we must cross the mountain together." If all went well that would be in about ten or eleven days time and I willingly agreed.

I went to bed wondering who it was that I was reminded of by Bruno. Was it an old friend who also had fought in World War II, albeit on the Allied side? Like Bruno, he lives his experiences with great intensity of purpose, as he had first demonstrated to me when we went to the Swiss Alps just one year after he had taken up rock climbing in middle age. There we had climbed a high mountain and he had thus fulfilled an ambition conceived in desperate wartime conditions in the desert. It had been a strand of hope linking him to a future after the conflict.

There were clear points of resemblance. Both could endure physical hardship, were subject to pendulum swings of mood and both were the most interesting and stimulating of companions. I smiled to myself in the darkness, imagining the conversations that Bruno and my friend the mountaineer might have had on such topics as war and religion. There was a degree of surrealistic humour in the idea that they might need my presence, during such discussions, to keep them in order.

I wakened, after the kind of sleep all foot travellers need, wondering if Bruno's interest in the Camino would end when he returned home. Could helping pilgrims become his life's work? Such was his faith, energy and commitment that I could see him harnessing these for such a cause. Might he become a latter-day Domingo? If I had been able to believe in reincarnation it would have been easy to see a link across the centuries.

After breakfast I left the hostal with Bruno in order to take his photograph. I asked him to fly his pennant from his rucksac and he did so, shyly, but willing to please me. We shook hands and I sat on one of the benches used by the old folk to watch the comings and goings, and gave him the chance to walk on alone.

In five minutes or so I followed and as I walked along a broad pedestrian area beside the road I was aware that its surface was laid out in coloured tiles as a map of the Road to Santiago. Every few metres was an illustration of another important town along the route, here Pamplona, then Estella and further on, Logrono. By the time I was at Santo Domingo, Bruno was already at Santiago. When I reached that stunning conclusion of the mosaic he was well out in front, head down, speeding along without the slightest sign of a backward look.

The day started damp and turned wet. I pushed on as fast as my blistered feet would allow, knowing from Bruno's notes that there was a good inn at Beldorado less than 25 kilometres away. The short stretch seemed a fair enough reward for the longer route of the previous day.

At some stage I must have passed Bruno in one of the villages without seeing him.

In the middle of the day I sat on a bank under a big tree at some distance from the road, resting and sheltering from the light, warm rain. I saw the now familiar figure of Bruno approaching. He was loping along, looking neither right nor left, taking no notice of either the weather or his surroundings.

As he drew level I knew that unless I shouted he would not see me on my sheltered perch. I opened my mouth to call out but thought the better of it as I remembered his wish to walk alone. To stop him here would break his reverie, so I watched the purposeful figure pressing on, pennant fluttering like a Tibetan prayer flag.

Suddenly I was aware that he was accompanied again. It was the same, slightly smaller figure in brown, keeping to his left, dodging along on the rough ground. I stood up for a better view and walked towards the road. Sure enough, my eyes told me what I knew was not possible. Bruno was not on his own.

Like many another mountaineer, I have sometimes had a feeling when travelling in mountains by myself, that I am not alone. It has never been an unpleasant or disconcerting experience, nor has there ever been a sense of having a companion. It has simply been a feeling of not being alone. Now for the first time I thought I could see a specific manifestation but linked with someone else.

The thought of telling sceptical friends about the incident made me smile and I went back to my seat under the tree, feeling much more cheerful than I had obvious reason to be.

When I had sat down, Bruno and his companion were out of sight and I was to see neither again on the Road to Santiago.

CHAPTER 7

Burgos

The rain fell steadily but lightly and gently, almost seeming to evaporate as it touched the skin and clothes. It was a relief when the old route of the Camino left the surfaced road and followed a track for a spell. Although there were few vehicles passing me on the road the verges were newly made and the rain had turned the soil to mud. It was bright yellow mud, the most sticky and clinging substance I had ever felt underfoot. It built up in layers under the sole like soft, wet snow balling under the heel on winter pavements.

A glance at the smaller scale map which covered a much larger stretch of country let me see that, after Burgos, the route struck out across country, miles from the main road. I seemed to remember that some of the writers had been less than enthusiastic about this section because of the heat, the barren countryside and the scarcity of settlements. For me it presented the most cheering prospect, the promise of open ground, of hillsides and plains and freedom from the sound, smell and menace of cars, coaches and juggernauts.

Beldorado appeared suddenly out of the dampness. The streets were wet and when I found the inn it was separated from the road by a large patch of open ground, partly cinder surfaced, pitted with potholes filled with rain water. I stepped between the muddy pools to the door of the inn and found the place open but un-attended.

The hallway was a litter of crates of empty bottles and cardboard boxes. It was scruffy and untidy, down-at-heel. I sat down on the bottom step of the stairs, content to wait, and once again feeling happier than circumstances justified.

Eventually the landlord arrived and showed me to my room. The first floor landing was in total contrast to the hallway below. It still held the appearance of a grand past, with good panelling in dark wood, fine plasterwork and an elegant little chandelier tinkling above the centre of the space. The bedroom was bright and clean, simply furnished and with a low comfortable-looking bed.

I unpacked my few possessions and sat on a chair at the window overlooking the damp, puddled cinder square. Across the road was a bus station and a small crowd was forming in anticipation of the next departure. I took off my shoes and socks and examined the soles of my feet. On one layers of skin had grown over the blister wound leaving a tough patch like fine leather. It was all I could have hoped for and was unlikely to give any further trouble. On the other sole there was still an open sore, slightly larger and deeper than before, as if the flesh was being peeled away. There was no sign of healing. It was still red, raw and oozing.

However, one sore foot is twice as good as two sore feet, and once again I carefully cleaned and dressed the wound in hope.

The landlord knocked at the door, a note in his hand which he had forgotten to give me when I arrived. It was from Bruno. It was harder for him to write English than speak it but the messages were clear. He had decided to go further that day, he wished me well and hoped we would meet at Astorga for the journey over the mountain.

"For Foncebadon" as he put it.

The name of the town, Beldorado, had been ringing in my ears since I had first seen it on the maps at the planning stage. Surely it was meant to be spoken aloud as two sounds, "Bel-Dorado". There had been no visual image in my mind but the sound had drawn me and in spite of the gloomy dampness of the day I was not disappointed. This was a town without the more obvious tourist attractions and thus could easily be ignored by travellers.

I had no conversations and only exchanged words when I needed to buy something but as the afternoon turned to evening the life and friendliness of the place unfolded around me. Without talking to the local people I felt welcome. Without visiting its notable buildings it seemed familiar. Its atmosphere was as calm and reassuring as a comfortable chair in a favourite room.

At nine o'clock I sat down to eat in the empty dining room of the inn. At this distance along the Road to Santiago there was no sinking feeling of loneliness at the prospect of eating alone yet again. The quietness of the room and my own silence seemed quite natural. Like the other facilities on the ground floor, the room had a threadbare, much used look about it. However, the tables were clean and the bread served in large slices in a wickerwork basket. The wine came, before I could even ask for it, in an earthenware jug which looked as if it had been steeped in a vat of dark red wine for a century.

The main course was merluza, which is hake or best quality cod. It had been lightly and carefully grilled to the point of tender, succulent perfection. It was served with a tossed green salad and a tomato salad and was perhaps the finest fish I have ever eaten.

It should have been a surprise to be eating so well in such a simple establishment but this was not so. The meal was entirely in keeping with Beldorado as I seemed to know it. If our expectations of the quality of food have been undermined by pretentious restaurant cuisine and mass catering, establishments like these inns are vital to the survival of good, simple food and country cooking.

As I ate, an old man entered the room leaning on a stick. He wore a large, blue beret and the clothes and boots of a farmer. The landlord and he were obviously well acquainted and as the man sat down and asked about the meal, a long argument began. As far as I could tell it was about the price of the meal and they harangued each other in fits and starts as the landlord passed the man's table. My impression was that the farmer got the best of the dealing, for as the host served he did so with a theatrical air of resignation. As soon as his back was turned the old man grinned gleefully across at me with his eyes narrowed and that look on his face which cattle dealers have when they know that they have won the best of the bargain.

We were too far apart to exchange words so we nodded to each other in friendly fashion. His meal arrived quickly, served in a casserole and accompanied by a large platter of green beans. He seemed to have the ability to eat and drink wine at the same time. I caught myself gaping at him in astonishment at this improbable talent and at the speed at which the food disappeared.

Afterwards I sat in a bright café in the main plaza. It was lively with young people in their late teens and twenties. Like the young in Santo Domingo they were dressed in the fashion of their age but here they were not a group apart. Although I exchanged with them only words of greeting, I knew I was welcome. At this stage it would have been a little easier for me to have conversed in Spanish and certainly some of them would have been able to speak English but they were leaving it to me to make a start and somehow the first words would not come. Those who lack inhibition in such circumstances find it hard to credit that others do not share their facility. I was not yet ready to do so.

The bar looked new and the equipment on the counter and attached to the wall behind it gleamed in chrome, glass and colourful plastic. The coffee machine on the bar itself fascinated me. It hissed and gurgled, almost jumping up and down on the counter in its enthusiasm to perform its function. Its animated activity fitted the lively scene exactly.

As I watched it exploded with a great crash and an eruption of steam. The bar emptied in seconds, the customers and staff afraid that there were more explosions to come. We stood on the pavement peering in through the big window and watching the vapour clear. The circular top had been blown off the cylinder of the machine and had risen like a rocket propelled missile to strike the ceiling and dislodge chunks of plaster.

The danger apparently over, we made our way back inside and the proprietor and his staff came around with free drinks and doughnuts to re-establish goodwill. The incident was enough to cause me to break silence but the chatter was now so excited that I found it almost impossible to understand what was being said.

A little later there were calls for coffee from the back of the bar but the look on the proprietor's face was clear indication that he was not ready to see the joke and that those who did were taking a chance with his temper.

I went to bed with the sound of the word Beldorado as I had heard the locals say it humming in my head. It had the distinctive inflections of Spain but vibrated like the Buddhist 'Ohm'; the sound of the world. It had the stilling power of a meditation mantra and sleep came gently and deep.

The morning's route was away from the surfaced road and led through beautiful countryside. There were wooded hills, the Montes de Oca, interspersed with farmland and carefully tended crops, fresh from the rain of the previous day, growing in the sunshine before my eyes. The clouds of yesterday had disappeared and the sun was hot but not uncomfortably so. Each time I crested a rise I found a breeze. It was the old Irish prayer again, "May the road always rise before you and the sun be on your back."

That was the way of it travelling through the Montes de Oca.

I came out on the main road for a spell and saw footprints in yesterday's mud at the verge. The tracks were Bruno's without doubt. It was the same sticky, gluey substance but firm enough now to show a clear print of a klettershue pattern, the type of boot he wore. The alternate steps were of unequal length and the imprints showed one foot pushing harder than the other. There was only one set of tracks.

The village of Villafranca - Montes de Oca is small and friendly, tucked into a cleft between the hills, with the inn at a twist in the road beside the river. Had it been further than the ten kilometres it was from Beldorado I would have been tempted to stay here as Bruno had done. Instead I sat down inside the inn for a rest in the shade.

The landlord greeted me as, 'El peregrino Irlandés' and I knew that Bruno had told him that I was a proper pilgrim, my own doubts notwithstanding. As far as Bruno was concerned I was within the brotherhood and there was nothing for it but to acquiesce. The title 'Irish' sat on me more easily. He could hardly be aware that in my corner of Ireland there are those who are Irish and those who are British and those who are either or neither as befits the occasion.

The miles sped by in the afternoon and Burgos, with its frantic city bustle of people and vehicles, was a shock to the system. Approached from the east the ancient part of the town is nowhere to be seen. The way to the centre seems blocked by modern office and apartment buildings, each one, according to its function, a replica of its neighbour. Interspersed are the prestige company buildings with grand facades and, no doubt, the standard office lay-out inside. It was frustrating and tiring trying to penetrate this commercial maze but the hope that Burgos might be as fine a city as I had been led to believe kept me searching.

Civilization, when I found it, was a small plaza near the cathedral. The buildings were a happy mixture of the old, the very old and the fairly recent. Directly opposite was one of recommended places of accommodation on Bruno's list. It was an imposing structure, holding on to its style and dignity, although obviously times were not as good as once they had been. The sign said "Hotel/Residencia" which I learned later meant that rooms and breakfast were available but not main meals.

The hallway was spacious and its antique furniture gleamed with years of careful polishing. The staff were courteous and friendly and the lift worked. Normally I would avoid, if at all possible, such mechanical means of ascent but my room was many floors up and my foot was a good excuse for taking advantage of the facility. My bedroom was large and comfortable and had a bathroom with shower. In Pamplona I had spent hours searching for somewhere like this to stay, now, with the assistance of Bruno's list, finding a most suitable place seemed so easy.

In spite of having a good base it took time to settle into the way of Burgos, to work out the plan of its streets, to find its true centre, that inner core which all cities worth visiting seem to have. But time was on my side. After ten days on the Camino I had planned to spend two nights in Burgos and have a full day's rest from walking, the first since leaving France.

In the evening I sat on a low circular wall which enclosed a large paved area with an ornate fountain at its centre. It was set in a plaza which drew me back time after time during my short stay in Burgos. Around the plaza were buildings of character, of a variety of periods. Some had pillars and colonnades and there were a few with ornate facades. The windows and balconies made a most pleasing pattern stretching from evening shadow to the last of the sunlight. At one side was a café in an old building but with a bright modern canopy over the pavement tables which confidently matched its setting.

At this time of the day the circular wall seemed to be for the adults, the paved area for children at play. These were the families of the locality enjoying the open air. They were ignoring the attraction of flickering images on television screens indoors to be out in the plaza where life itself was the entertainment.

The children were chasing and playing ball, dodging and jumping, shouting and pushing bu all in fun and without the need for adult

THE CAMINO FRANCÉS
FROM ST JEAN PIED-DE-PORT TO SANTIAGO

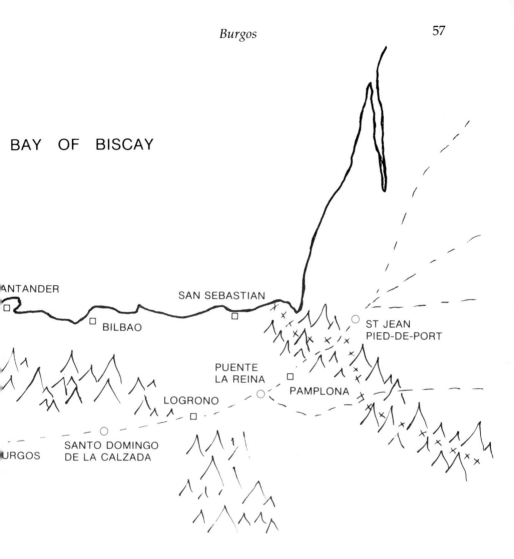

BAY OF BISCAY

ANTANDER

SAN SEBASTIAN

BILBAO

ST JEAN
PIED-DE-PORT

PUENTE
LA REINA

LOGRONO

PAMPLONA

SANTO DOMINGO
DE LA CALZADA

URGOS

SPAIN

interference. The game which required the most serious approach involved stepping over and between two long, elastic strands held in tension around two of the players. It required rhythm and grace and was performed with great skill by some of the older girls, those around twelve or thirteen years of age.

The adults conversed and gossiped, keeping an eye on their own particular charges. It would be hard for a city to find a place for me the way Beldorado had managed to do but Burgos was doing its best. Perhaps changes in my own attitudes were enabling this to happen. It was as if a journey like this allowed the traveller to feel the heart beat of the settlements on its route.

I went back to the Hotel/Residencia in cheerful good humour feeling as if I had been in Burgos for a week.

Next day I went to the cathedral early to see its spires against the morning sun and found its light shining through them. The tall structures looked too delicate and finely cut to be made of stone. Inside there were iron-grilled and gated chapels in alcoves around the walls, some with tables prepared for mass. Almost the whole of the central area was closed in as if it were a church within a church, a place for special devotions. I knew this to be a famous cathedral held in the highest regard and I found it huge, intricate and impressive. On the outside I could appreciate it as a religious symbol of great beauty but inside it was too complex for me to unravel or understand.

I sat in the sunshine at a pavement café with a whole day of rest stretching before me and ordered sweet Burgos cakes with my coffee. It might be a most interesting city but, apart from resting, my most serious task was to eat. In ten days on the Road I knew I had used more energy walking than I had replaced by food taken in through snacks and meals. It had been hard to eat as much as I felt was necessary mainly because of the heat and the lateness of the evening meal. When little is eaten for a few days the capacity to take in food seems to reduce rapidly. As I enjoyed the cakes there was a certain wry humour in the idea that, although I had to eat, some of those at other tables might be feeling guilty at their own indulgence.

On inspection Burgos proved more spacious and better laid-out than my first impression would have indicated. The streets were clean and well kept. Beside the river was a wide pedestrian area with trees planted amongst the mosaic paving. Having yet another rest and a coffee I was again able to watch the dancing game involving the elastic strands.

A girl of about twelve was playing while her mother took coffee with a friend at a table near mine. The elastic bands were attached above knee height to two convenient trees. The girl hummed softly and clapped in a double rhythm as she stepped and kicked her way over and between the strands. The time and phasing changed in a pattern so complex that I could only recognise it in snatches. At intervals she would stop to rehearse a step and then start again into the full routine. The most intricate stage was reached when she kicked a foot to entangle it in one strand then turned with a jump to face the other way and so wrap both strands around both legs. Extrication looked impossible but still humming, clapping and hopping she gave a twist and by sleight of leg she was released. It was like the game we played as children which we called Cat's Cradle, threading string between the fingers and then with one quick jerk freeing both cord and hands.

For half an hour or more the girl played in her own time, concentrating on the rhythm and the skill, looking for no praise or encouragement, delighting in the repetition of the familiar.

As I explored the city and rested by turns, the day slipped by. For the second time I failed to find a good place to eat in the evening. It may well have been my own fault.

Burgos looked as if it might be famous for its food. In the shops the meat, fish, vegetables and fruit appeared to be of the finest quality. In the windows there were pyramids of cheeses and over the counters, hanging on rails were lines of neatly labelled hams and chorizo sausages. At mid-day the bars displayed such an array of appetising tapas that I accepted the challenge and sampled as many as I could manage.

Perhaps the best were the sardines, lightly fried but with crisp skins. In many countries the sardine is a tiny fish available in a tin. The Spanish sardina can be as big as a small herring. It is grilled or fried in hot oil and served whole. With Spanish bread and a little wine it was as perfect a light meal as I could wish for.

Travelling on foot could hardly be deemed essential to the appreciation of the simple wines of a country, but it helps prevent pretension. In the Codex Calixtinus, Amery Picaud's recommendations were stated clearly and frankly and would, no doubt, have been appreciated by the pilgrims of that time. On my brief visit I found the wines of Burgos still eminently drinkable.

I visited the plaza I now thought of as the Peoples' Square and as the evening reached towards night the excited chatter there turned to quiet conversation. Gradually the games and skipping ceased as some families drifted away and children joined their parents on the low wall and listened with serious faces to the talk of grown-ups.

With a series of long days ahead I wanted my rest day to end early and as this part of the city closed itself down for the night I walked back to the Hotel/Residencia.

I slept well but not the deep, untroubled sleep of Puente la Reina in the room as calm and quiet as a deep well. Here the dreams were of complicated arrangements and involved explanations. It was not an unpleasant experience even though the animated, agitated images

Pilgrims' Footsteps

crowded against each other. It would have been interesting to have noted
the details immediately on wakening. The happy result was that I rose
and packed in optimistic mood, un-worried even about the foot that was
sure to give me trouble as soon as I started.

It was a most impressive way to leave Burgos, through the cloisters
of the cathedral, under the Santa Maria Arch in the city wall and across
the Matatos Bridge.

On the other side of the river I looked back and, if my first sight of the
city from the east had been of a depressing maze of concrete buildings,
from the south the balance was more than redressed. Here there was, in
one field of view, a glimpse of the history of the city, set in stone. The
bridge pointed directly at the arched gate-way in the walls and perched
above was the dramatic skyline of the tower and spires of the cathedral.
A last impression can overwhelm a first.

For the ten kilometres from Burgos to the village of Tardajos the old
road and the modern highway follow the same route, with one brief
divergence. It was a Saturday morning and the traffic was light but the
day became warm much earlier than usual and a main road is no place
to be walking on a hot week-end.

Tardajos had been an important objective for many days. At this point
the traditional route of the pilgrim camino and the modern road separate.
They do not meet again until near the city of Leon, well over one hundred
and sixty kilometres away. This was a part of the route which Walter
Starkie and many illustrious pilgrims before him had found dull.
However it was obvious from the map that from here the Camino was
still a path over open countryside with occasional stretches on lanes and
country roads. Neither the distance nor the adverse remarks of my
predecessors could prevent me looking forward to being away from
main roads and their traffic for a week. The prospect of strolling, or
striding, across the hills and plains was just the encouragement I needed.

At the very point where I was leaving the main road there was a café
and I decided to celebrate my imminent release from competition with
mechanically propelled vehicles by having a cool drink and a coffee.

The barman was pleased to see a stranger. He tried a variety of
languages and was even more pleased when he found I could speak
English.

"Two years I lived in London." he said, "Worked in a bar. No English
ever come here, only French and German." He grimaced and shrugged
as he mentioned both these nationalities.

"London is good for work." he said as he served me. "I want to go
back, but how will I sell this?" He gestured with both arms outstretched
and his faint air of contempt for his premises could not have been justified
by the clean, modern interior.

Burgos: The Santa Maria Arch.

FIRMA DE LA ESPAGNE
EN C.E.E.
("YES TO SPAIN IN THE E.E.C.")

It was a wonderful, colourful event, a happy celebration that everyone seemed to be enjoying. I stayed up as long as I could and went to bed after eleven o'clock. The festival proper started soon afterwards with music and the sound throbbed across the countryside.

It was not in the expectation of sleep that I lay down on that comfortable bed but in the real need of rest. The day's walk had been glorious but the distance, and the sore foot, and the pain in the hip had left me weary. Physical tiredness, except to an extreme degree is not unpleasant in the way that mental or emotional tiredness can be, but there comes a point when the body knows it needs rest.

Outside there was all the clamour of the circus with its side shows and that special kind of music that seems part of the show where ever they play to the world. A rock band took to the platform and their sound tried to dominate the festivities. The wall of the bedroom shook to the beat, it must have made the whole village vibrate.

Stretched out on the bed I relaxed in the luxury of rest. I felt no resentment at the clamour and the unlikelihood of being able to sleep. I was the stranger. The locals were entitled to hold their fiesta when they chose and if this was the form they wanted it to take then that was their affair. I was glad to have shared their fun for a little while and now to have a comfortable bed. In other circumstances I might have reacted in a totally different way but here in Castrojeriz I rested easily.

I must have dozed from time to time for at five thirty I was startled awake by the silence, the rock band had ceased to play. The circus had closed down and the dancing stopped with the music. The main crowd began to leave for home and there were only a few stragglers left. These were the same grimly determined remnants left behind by celebrations all over the world, the rearguard, sticking it out to the bitter end.

At seven-thirty I arose and could hear the last of the revellers singing their way home. For the first time there was silence and, having paid the previous evening, I let myself out of the sleeping building. The whole village was asleep, even the animals were taking the opportunity to make up for a missed night's rest.

A side street took me towards a range of low hills called El Rebollar over which I knew the route lay. To the north was Castrojeriz Peña, the hill of Castrojeriz, with battlements at its summit. The day was bright but not sunny and I plodded along half-asleep and left the road for the track which led to the hills.

Beyond Castrojeriz.

An ancient stone causeway stretched across marshy ground to the foot of El Rebollar. The path climbed steeply up the flank of the range and it was worn through the soil and rubble to the bed-rock of the hill.

After an hour or so I stopped at a crest of a rise to make breakfast, feeling that I had travelled far enough on one drink of water. The little gas stove brought the water to boil for coffee and I set out the biscuits, fruit and cheese. As the shops were closing for the fiesta the previous evening I had managed to buy a few provisions and at this moment they looked like a feast. The fruit looked particularly succulent, there were two large pears and four peaches but they would have to do me until late evening. The biscuits were a crisp, butter variety which were cheap, excellent and available everywhere. The coffee was made from instant powder, of course, but in such a place the flavour was good.

I looked down the way I had come and followed the line of the track across the causeway and back to the valley of Castrojeriz. A few animals were grazing in a far away field but there was no sign of human life as I scanned a great sweep of countryside from my perch. The braying of a single donkey reached me from the valley, the insistent, raucous call of man's most under-rated friend. Was it the same donkey who had led last night's parade, annoyed that the fun was over?

I packed the stove and the remainder of the food into the rucksac and moved on up the track. The short distance I had put between myself and the village seemed to have separated me from Castrojeriz by time. It was less than two hours since I had heard the last of the revellers rolling home, now the fiesta seemed to have happened days before.

As I travelled over the hills of El Rebollar I felt that, as my legs did the walking, my mind was still asleep, dreaming that I was on the move. The hills were higher than the meseta but once at the crest the route swept gently downwards to cross the sizable Rio Pisuerga by a road bridge.

It was a relief to find an inn in Formista. Bruno's notes had not indicated that there was one but when I reached the Postada, yet another word for an inn, I knew that I had travelled far enough for the day. The route had been another wonderful section of the old Camino and the only real problem, not the lack of sleep, but the wound on the sole of one foot. It was becoming larger and more painful by the day. The sore and its surround were so inflamed and tender that I could hardly bear to touch it for cleaning purposes. It had now become a worry lest it should prevent me finishing the journey.

The Postada was in a quiet plaza away from the main road. It was one of a row of houses and was as small and compact as the dwellings. The children of the household sat on the front doorstep playing a little game

Church at Formista.

with fingers and palms and as I arrived they stood up to let me enter. A young one ran past me calling to her mother that someone had arrived.

It was the middle of the afternoon and I showered and lay down on the bed for a rest before seeing the town. Nearby was the church of San Martin built in the eleventh century and therefore as old as the pilgrimage itself. I had read that it was the finest example of Romanesque architecture in Spain. It seemed appropriate to the pilgrim road that the church should be here, hidden in this remote part of the country, well off the tourist routes.

It was a sturdy, compact building with two round towers at the front corners and a larger, square tower with chamfered corners at the rear. The stone was the colour of old gold and the roof tiles a faded russet-red. This was not a church designed to look like a small cathedral but a place of worship in its own right. Its presence, proportions and colour made it one of the most pleasing buildings I have ever seen. Of its interior I saw nothing for it was a Sunday afternoon and it is closed in the afternoons of both Saturday and Sunday.

There were four of us for the evening meal in the tiny dining room of the inn. My three companions were men in their fifties or sixties and they greeted me in Spanish. As they ordered the meal one of them turned to me as if the idea had just occurred to him.

"We are French." he said in the kind of grand tone that suits that language so well. " We are going to Santiago."

It was delivered as a statement not to be taken lightly. I was aware that they spoke French for I had heard them chatting as they ordered but it was still a mild surprise to be addressed in that tongue.

"Me too." I replied in their language and they stood up to shake hands in formal fashion. We introduced ourselves and they nodded gravely when they learned that I was from Ireland.

They invited me to join them at their table and as I did so I placed my bread and wine beside theirs. There was a pause as if we were deciding which language to use for conversation. I broke the silence in English.

"The Three French Gentlemen." I said. One of them smiled broadly, translating with a courtier's gesture of the hand for the benefit of the others and all three looked suitably complimented.

The one who could speak English could do so quite well and, during the meal, we conversed in that language. They were close friends who lived in different parts of France and whose practice was to go on holiday together.

The oldest was tall and slightly stooped and proud to be active enough at sixty-five years of age to be able to keep up with his younger companions. My guess was that he was a retired civil servant with a great variety of interests. He would be silent for long periods and then make his own special, precise contribution expecting to be listened to with serious attention.

The youngest was fifty-three, a short, stocky, powerful looking man with close-cropped grey hair and a quiet, courteous manner which belied his robust appearance. He spoke no English at all.

The third was a lean and active sixty-three year old. He was the one who spoke English and, although he was never allowed by his friends to give the impression that he might be the leader of the group, his linguistic ability meant that he led our conversations.

They too had started at St. Jean Pied-de-Port in France and had been a week longer on the Camino. It was their practice to keep Sunday as a rest day and to take other rest days when they felt the need. As we exchanged experiences I found that they had met Bruno. It had only been a brief encounter and they had little to say about him.

They were intrigued to discover that I had not known of the existence of the organisation in Paris which helped pilgrims and very interested in the way that I had worked out the route from old books and traced it on large scale maps.

The eldest may have been an ex-army man for he pored over my maps with the pleasure of an expert.

When I told them of the blister wound on my foot they offered me a remedy called Second Skin. Like a slightly injured mountaineer aware of the fuss caused by his rescue, I was embarrassed about accepting help. I had never been impressed by blister remedies and, as politely as possible, I declined.

After the meal I went out into the plaza in front of the Postada for a breath of fresh air. Three young girls were playing the dancing game with the strands of elastic.

"¿Cómo se llama?" I said, pleased to be able to ask what it was called.

"Goma" said the eldest and politely took my pen and note-book to print the words on the back cover.

Next morning I left the inn after the three Frenchmen and gave them a good start. It was not too far to Carrion de los Condes but I was becoming more worried that the foot wound would stop me in my tracks. If this was to be the day, I wanted to be behind them when it happened.

Much of the route lay along lanes and narrow country roads and the drivers of the occasional vehicles which passed slowed down and waved cheerily. The verges on either side were waist high with wild flowers, great banks of blue, yellow and white blooms swaying gently in the light airs. Walking through such beauty kept the pain at bay.

Pilgrims' Footsteps

I reached Carrion de los Condes at mid-day and found, in the main plaza, the café recommended in Bruno's notes as providing accommodation. The Frenchmen had arrived before me and we were offered two double rooms between the four of us. I left them to share the rooms and, with some difficulty, found one for myself above a restaurant in a quiet street some distance away.

Carrion is at the centre of an important agricultural region and has the quietly prosperous air of a successful market town. For lunch I went back to a small fonda which provided meals but not accommodation and where I had received crucial help in finding a room.

The dining room was well furnished and appointed and looked much more spacious than it was. There were three customers whom I took to be local business people and regulars and a young man intent on having a celebration even though he was alone. When the orders had been taken I gathered from the cross talk that he was a salesman who had obtained an important order that morning. He toasted the rest of us in the room and we raised our glasses to him. I smiled and nodded encouragingly, hoping that I had understood correctly.

The meal was served with great care and to me, as a stranger, with some pride. It was the simplest of restaurant meals but prepared, cooked and served by people who understood food and cared for its quality. The entire staff seemed to be the proprietress and her daughter and at the end of the meal they both came to the dining room to thank us shyly for honouring them with our custom.

In the heat of the afternoon I sat in the shady side of the main plaza knowing that the next day's route was long and difficult. The blister sore was becoming steadily worse. It was now too painful to touch even to clean. I had to face the depressing prospect that to-morrow would surely see the end of my journey on foot: that I would have to find some other form of transport if I was to continue. I decided to leave that problem to the morning, to make an early start as usual and let the day bring what it would.

Facing me across the plaza was the Santiago church. It was a solid lump of a building with a stocky tower which seemed to hold it together. On its own it might have been an ugly structure but here in the centre of the town with the houses built against it on either side, there was no question but that it was the right church in the right place. Should it ever be removed the whole town will fall down.

Between the arch of the doorway and the lower line of the roof is a frieze, worked in stone and running the length of the building. It was carved in the 12th century to illustrate the pilgrimage and has survived the years well, setting off this simple place of worship in a remarkably impressive way.

I crossed the plaza to the bar where the Frenchmen were in residence. They were surrounded by locals, three or four of whom were loudly offering advice on the Camino at the same time and, I gathered later from the Frenchmen, trying to involve them in rounds of drinking. I was greeted with relief.

"Thank you for coming back." said the Frenchman who spoke English, "You must save us from our new friends."

With sighs and shrugs he explained that there was to be a fiesta in Carrion that evening, right here in the plaza under their bed-rooms. The locals had already started to celebrate and were insisting that the visitors join in. I ordered coffee for the four of us at a table at the back of the bar and they thanked me with obvious admiration for this sound tactical move. Knowing that already they had doubts about the degree of seriousness with which I was approaching the pilgrimage, I wagged a finger at them in admonishment and said severely, first in English and then in the best French I could muster.

"Nothing must be allowed to keep the pilgrim from the Road."

Before we parted we agreed to meet early that evening to look for somewhere to eat. The youngest went upstairs to his room and returned with the Second Skin treatment for blisters. He reached it to me without a word and I guessed he had seen me walk across the plaza to the café.

On the way back to my room I read the instructions, found that I needed adhesive surgical tape and bought a roll of it at a chemists. The instructions were simple. A piece of the Second Skin material should be cut to cover the wound and fastened in place with surgical tape.

I pulled a chair close to the bed and set out the necessary items on a clean towel, the scissors, the surgical tape, antiseptic powder and, of course, the Second Skin. The smaller blisters on each foot had cleared up long since leaving the skin thicker to prevent further trouble. The large blister on the sole of the right foot had healed cleanly with concentric rings to show the layers of skin which had been worn through.

It was the left foot which needed treatment and I cleaned it carefully. The Second Skin was a thin layer of a jelly-like substance, held between strips of fine plastic and kept moist in a sealed container. The hole on the left sole was worn through the skin layers to expose a raw, red and oozing patch of flesh. It took seconds only to apply the Second Skin and the tape. I put on a clean sock and a training shoe and stood up. There was no pain. I put on the other sock and shoe and took a few steps. Sure enough the pain had gone.

I had intended to lie down for a rest but that was forgotten. I hurried outside to try the feel of the pavement. It was a minor miracle. For the first time in almost a fortnight I could walk without pain. I dodged a passer-by with what felt like a neat, rugby side-step and went for a little stroll just for the pleasure of it. There was no sign of the soreness in the hip and no need to worry about limping. The energy seemed to flow back into the legs. It was a moment of huge relief.

The prudent side of me counselled caution, encouraging me to wait until the end of the next day's long stage before I raised my expectations too high. But the fact was that I could face the morning with hope that I still might be able to finish the journey on my own two feet.

It was only at this moment, when the concern had gone, that I realised how worried I had been that this simple injury would stop me.

I called on the Three French Gentlemen at their rooms to return the package of Second Skin and they insisted that I take enough of it to last for a few days. I did so, wrapping it carefully in plastic to prevent drying out.

That evening the four of us searched the town for somewhere to eat but every possible place was closed or on the point of so doing. We combed the streets at speed, asking and looking. Although we were having no success, we were all in high spirits. My reason was obvious, at least to me, and it seemed to be the searching itself which had brought them to life.

The eldest, who was striding out in front at one stage like a long-legged running bird, suddenly stopped and turned to face us.

"The Three Musketeers," he said in French, "Now are complete with D'Artagnan." He doffed his woolly hat with a grand sweep of the arm as if it had been a fine chapeau with broad brim and plume, and bowed low in my direction. We laughed and pointed him onwards, telling him to stop his foolery and find us somewhere to eat.

Our searching sweeps took us to the edge of the town and the eldest, who was still in the lead gave a shout of triumph. He had found a bar with tapas laid out in dishes on the counter. As we entered he raised an arm and asked us to be calm.

"Sit down please." he said in the tones of authority. "I will order. Age must have some privilege."

He went to speak to the staff and when he returned produced with a flourish, from behind his back, two carafes of red wine. "We drink little" he said to me, still in French "And even less in Spain. But success must be celebrated."

The meal, when it arrived, was on two large trays. Our friend had simply asked the barman to deliver all the dishes of tapas on the counter to our table. There were three kinds of grilled small fish, half a round of potato omelette, hard boiled eggs stuffed with anchovies, a dish of mushrooms in garlic and a pile of meat balls, freshly cooked and smelling of herbs - rosemary - I thought, and a bowl of black olives.

"Et vous aussi." I said. "Bon voyage."

I shook hands with The Three French Gentlemen and left them as I had found them in serious contemplation of what they should or should not eat.

CHAPTER 9

The Belgian Boys Walk to Freedom

Although it was almost nine o'clock and the morning was fresh and cool after the heat of the previous day, Sahagun had not yet come to life. The road crossed the Rio Cea and I walked on the tree-lined verge. A second small piece of the Second Skin was now in place and for a second day I was stepping on a small miracle.

Perhaps it seems odd to have made so much of a mere blister but travelling this way means many hours spent on the feet each day. The distances may be long and the paths rough. Even worse, there may be smooth surfaces where the same part of the foot strikes the ground, step after step. Once a blister begins there is nothing for it but to treat it well, keep it clean and accept the pain. With the arrogance of experience I had refused the Frenchmen's offer of the patent treatment at the first time of asking. Having had a day to think about it and yet another day to thole the pain, it was easy to swallow the expert's pride and accept the help offered.

After a few kilometres I left the road at a small village and followed a yellow arrow pointing along a path. It led to a range of low hills some distance away and, as usual, my spirits rose as the route climbed.

This is a part of the Camino which follows a line well away from the main road. The villages are connected to each other by paths and jeep tracks and, by a wider well-maintained track, to the surfaced road. Some of the remote settlements have names which announce their connection with the Pilgrimage. One of these is called Bercianos del Real Camino but there are obvious alternative tracks and I was heading away from that village towards the trees at the very crest of the range. On the higher ground there were scattered copses linked to each other by single trees and little groups of bushes.

As far as I could see the countryside was empty of people. The only habitation was a rambling hacienda on a small estate. The ancient gates were open but there was no sign of the occupants or their animals. It seemed odd that there was not even a dog to bark at the stranger. I checked the large scale map and the estate was named, Valdelocajos.

Further on I sat down under a tree to heat water for a cup of coffee and to rest in the shade. I was a little way from the path and it was a comfortable vantage point. The tree was at a good angle to lean back against and I had a view over a great stretch of country which sloped gently to the south-east towards the hazy plain way below me.

There was a scuffling noise on the path and I turned to see two boys swinging along from the direction I had come, heads down, carrying large rucksacs, travelling quickly in spite of the heat. I recognised them as the lads I had met two days before on the way to Carrion de los Condes. That day I had been taking a break at the side of the road and they had come over a rise walking quickly, slightly bent forward under their loads. They had stopped for a few moments when I greeted them and we had exchanged a few words, without giving anything away about ourselves. At the time I had accepted their abrupt shyness as the awkwardness many young people seem to show when meeting someone older.

Now I had a chance to study them before they saw me. They were eighteen or nineteen years of age, wearing shorts and denim wasistcoats without shirts. Their hair was longish and unruly after the fashion of many young Northern Europeans and their faces were set in effort. The nearer one was spectacularly tattooed on the upper arm and the other wiped the sweat from his brow with a white rag. My guess was that they were Danish.

"Buenos Dias!" I shouted and they startled, so unexpected was it to hear someone call out before they saw him. I waved and, when they saw who it was, they came over to greet me like old friends. There was no shyness now.

"You too go to Santiago?" one of them asked in English. I nodded and smiled at the warmth of their approach and at the very idea of being asked the question by these unlikely-looking pilgrims. Here we were in a remote corner of the Province of Leon discovering that we were all bound for Santiago, still over three hundred and forty kilometres away.

"Yes" I said "I am also on the Camino." The boys grinned, made themselves comfortable in the shade and I reached them the packet of biscuits.

It seems a first principle of communication that the parties must share, at the very least, some facility in a common language. Even more important however, is the desire to understand and be understood. With only a few words and phrases in English and French, and the use of gestures, finger signs, facial expressions, drawings in the dust and uninhibited ham-acting we managed very well. Much better, it must be said, than I had done on the last evening with The Three French Gentlemen.

I discovered that they were from a Dutch-speaking part of Belgium and they nodded wisely, as if understanding its full significance, when I told them that home for me was Northern Ireland.

We scrutinised each other's maps and hefted the rucksacs to feel what the others had to carry. By comparison mine seemed so light that never again on the trip did I feel it was much of a weight to carry.

I drew a tent in the dust and mimed the knee-high mist to tell them that I had seen a tent on the river bank the morning I had left Carrion de los Condes. Proudly they indicated that it had been their tent and mimed the fact that they had still been fast asleep. I gathered too, it had been after a late night. Unlike The Frenchmen and myself they had attended the fiesta and had certainly enjoyed themselves.

The feeling that we were part of a brotherhood of the road was tangible. The age and language gaps were gone. It was of no account that we had still so far to go, for we had such a long way behind us. That distance was now a bond.

Initial curiosity satisfied and friendship established the boys shook hands with me and rose to go.

"See you on the Camino." I said, it took them a moment and a little discussion to work out what I meant. They grinned.

"See you on the Camino." they replied and shouldered their rucksacs. I watched them move quickly down the track towards the plain and the hottest part of the day.

Packing was easy, there was so little for me to pack. I swung the rucksac gently over the shoulder and left the shade of the trees into the full glare of the sun. The boys were nowhere to be seen and I made good time without trying to hurry. Once on the plain it was easier to keep going than to stop for an occasional rest, for without shade there were no attractive places to pause.

Ahead I saw a huge flock of sheep eating their way slowly across the countryside. They were following a shepherd who strolled at a most leisurely pace. He was a stocky, elderly man, dressed in black and keeping comfortable under a large black umbrella. His four dogs bounded towards me and it was a relief to find them friendly. I had not expected to meet dogs so far from the villages and was not carrying a stick. Three of the dogs were like collies and they sniffed around me busily. The fourth was a great hound of a size that would once have been necessary to protect the flock. Perhaps this was still his function. Shepherds at work are not known for taking dogs with them as pets. The hound wandered up to me expecting a pat and his master stopped, hoping for a chat.

The collies loped off to circle around the sheep in case they strayed too far and the hound sat down to watch. It was possible for me to feel the shepherd's interest in me as a traveller before he began to speak. He told me that it was a hot day. He shook his umbrella at the sky as if defying the sun's rays and at the same time showing me that he was well prepared. Our conversation developed in easy stages as he made a simple statement and changed it into a question by raising his voice at the end of the sentence. It was the first time on the journey that I had exchanged in Spanish more than a greeting or a few words in a shop or an inn.

"You travel alone?" he asked and I tried to use his words as I replied.

"Yes, I travel alone." I said. He asked about the journey, my destination, how far I had come, the number of days I had been on the Camino.

Although I had far less familiarity with the language than French, it was already much easier to talk to this gentle countryman in his own tongue than it had been to converse with the Frenchmen. He came back to the fact that I was on my own and I was aware that a shepherd would know more than most of us about being alone. He asked if I would not have liked a friend to walk with me and I had the double difficulty of deciding what to answer and finding the Spanish words to fit.

"Sometimes when I stop," I said "It would be good to have a friend to talk to." If the words were coming slowly, in little phrases, it was no harm. He nodded in understanding and encouragement and I continued, "But on the Camino I like to walk by myself." In very deliberate fashion he nodded again, this time in approval.

The shepherd pointed towards a village in the distance and told me its name, "Calzadilla de los Hermanillos." I said the words after him to try to sound them his way. He smiled and told me that beyond the village was the wonderful city of Leon.

We shook hands and I left him with his flock and dogs and headed towards Calzadilla. After a few minutes I looked back and he was still standing in the same place, watching me on my way. He raised his umbrella high and gave it a shake. It was a gesture of exultation and I could not help feeling a little surge of pride. It seemed important that this old man should be so well disposed towards me and my journey.

The path led to Calzadilla and I entered the village by its back door. It was the early afternoon and there was no sign of life except at a small bar near the road which connected the village to the rest of the world. Behind the counter was a boy with a withered arm who smiled but did not speak when I entered. As I drank cold orange juice from his refrigerator, he made a coffee for me with great speed and dexterity using his one good hand. It was obvious that he was waiting for me to speak first. I told him as best I could that I hoped to spend the night at the next village and travel on to Leon the next day. This released a torrent of helpful information and advice, delivered with such enthusiasm that I had to ask him to say it all again, slowly. He traced the route with a finger on my map and told me that there was an inn at the village in which I hoped to stay. Like the shepherd, he was full of praise for Leon. He had been there many times, he said. It was the most beautiful city in Spain.

When it was time for me to leave he came out with me to make sure I was on the right track. As with the shepherd, I had probably given him something to talk about over the next few days or weeks. If the old man came to his bar for a drink I wondered if they would compare impressions when they discovered I had met them both. Each in his own way had helped me on my journey more than they would know.

The next stage to El Burgo Ranero was through open country without shade. It was the hottest day so far and it would have been more sensible to have waited in Calzadilla until the late afternoon. However, once started on the way there is a desire to keep going and, on this stretch, no turning back.

I reached the railway line and had to make a detour to cross it by a bridge. It was a struggle up the little incline and I realised that I was more tired than I had been before. The lack of energy was partly a result of travelling in the heat but it seemed clear now that I was not eating enough to provide sufficient fuel for the journey. Once again I resolved to eat more.

At the edge of the village I had to sit down on a low wall to rest. It was not in the shade but I felt I could go no further. The village straggled out across the countryside with gaps between groups of buildings as if it might once have been a cluster of settlements. As I got my bearings I saw that there was a café close by and struggled to it to rest in the shade and drink glasses of cold orange juice. In spite of my resolution I could eat nothing.

The girl in charge was obviously part of the attraction of the establishment and she had the full attention of the three male customers present. Their smart cars were outside on the dirt road and they looked like well-dressed travelling men from the city. I guessed that the girl was the reason that each of them was lunching here. She might easily have been flattered by the impression she was having on them but, if she was aware of this effect, she ignored it. She chatted to the dusty stranger, sweat-streaked and travel-weary though he was and told him that the inn was at the other end of the village about one kilometre away. I took my leave and left her to her suitors.

It was the longest kilometre so far and, when I reached the inn, lunch was still being served although it was after three o'clock. Two men were seated in the dining room at separate tables each surrounded by the debris of a substantial meal and we nodded in greeting. The inn was tiny, a small house run by a senora, lowset, dressed in black and of very considerable energy. She showed me to my room and asked me not to sleep in the middle bed. At first I thought that it had been booked for another customer. Then I realised that she was warning me that its legs were bad and that if I sat on it they would collapse. She assumed that I would want lunch and told me to take my time having a shower, lunch would wait for me.

Half an hour later I came down refreshed and hungry. The meal began with a great tureen of soup and I remembered Bruno's advice. "Always we must have soup." he would say. "The peregrino must have much liquid." He was right of course. I took my time enjoying the home-made broth and lamented the growing popularity of tinned and packeted soups, even in countries where cooks should know better.

The main course was merluza and I had to marvel how fish could be so fresh and succulent in a remote village like this. The senora filled the wine jug each time I poured myself a glassful. It was a light red colour, a clean and refreshing accompaniment to the food. As she filled the jug on one occasion, I startled her by laughing quietly to myself. It seemed necessary to explain in case she might be offended so I made a special effort to get it right.

"In my country," I said in Spanish, "People drink . . ." I was stuck for the next few words and to fill the space she repeated my last phrase and waited, anxious not to rush me. Then I thought I had the words. "Vino blanco solo con pescados." I said and hoped the sentence meant, "In my country people drink only white wine with fish."

It was obviously close enough. She looked at the wine jug remembering that she had refilled it and began to laugh.

"Pero hombre!" she said "Pero hombre!!" for which, I suppose, there is an equivalent in English, for now however the sound of "But man!" was eloquence enough. She shook her head from side to side still laughing at the folly of those who would only drink white wine with fish.

Before I went to my room for a siesta the senora told me that dinner would be at ten-thirty that evening. By this stage I saw nothing odd in eating so late, it seemed to fit the pattern of the day.

After an hour's rest in the cool of the room I set out to tour the village and to find a café where I could, as usual, celebrate my safe arrival with a cool drink.

Most of the houses were old and of a similar style to those in Calzadilla. It was an unusual and distinctive type of construction. The houses were built of bricks made from mud and straw and surfaced with a plaster also made from mud. One was in the course of construction so it was possible to see the method. Nearby was a large pond surrounded by mud flats and it was evident that this was where the bricks were made.

A finished house was a shade of light brown and looked as if it might have been baked in a kiln. The older buildings had weathered to the colour of the earth itself like the village of Hontanas all those days behind me.

There was one large structure with an ancient tower and perched precariously near its top was a great untidy nest. Two large birds were in residence and as they stood up I could see that they were storks.

In the village square almost everywhere was closed. The houses were shuttered and the shops shut. Standing in the shadow of a doorway was a young man watching me closely. He was tall and thin, dressed like a farm worker. I asked him for directions to the bar and he shook his head as if he was unable to understand me. I tried again and he put his head on one side and repeated the word "Bar, bar, bar, bar . . ." like the beat of a drum. He beckoned me to follow and led the way with a slow hopping run, moving sideways as if to make sure that I was following. We came to a corner and he stood on one leg, pointing around it. As he skipped and hopped back to his original place I looked around the corner but could see no sign of the bar.

I turned back towards the square but my guide stopped me and I followed him along a narrow street to the edge of the village and the pond. Beside the mud flats was a dilapidated building only recognisable as a bar by reason of a sign which simply enough said "Bar". My guide hopped up and down with pleasure when he saw me focus on my objective and left at speed before I could thank him.

The bar looked as if it was in the process of falling down. It must have taken many years of neglect to achieve its present state but work was in progress. The two young Belgians were stripped to the waist and chipping at a window ledge with chisels and masons' hammers. I watched as they tried to fit a beautiful marble sill to the ledge and wondered if the wall would be strong enough to support it.

I greeted them in Spanish and they downed tools, waving me over with shouts of welcome. Inside, the bar looked much better than it did on the outside. There was no one to serve so one of the boys fetched me a beer from the refrigerator.

"Our friend is here." one of the boys said in a mixture of English and French, leading me to a side door. "Johannes." he said pointing at a sandy-haired, bearded man sitting astride a chair carving a large wooden head. I introduced myself and he stood up to shake hands.

"The boys have told me about you." he said smiling and speaking in very good English.

Behind him on the window-sill was a clay figure of a pilgrim a little over a foot high. It was well modelled in traditional garb but the legs had obviously been damaged and repaired roughly.

"I see you have another companion." I said nodding at the clay figure. "Did he have an accident on the Camino?"

Johannes stretched upright from his work and laughed. He pointed with his chisel.

"Our friend fell as he was crossing the Pyrenees." he said, "Both his legs were broken and I have not yet fixed them properly."

For an hour or more we talked quietly and I enjoyed the luxury of easy, interesting conversation. The boys went back to work and the young man who had guided me to the bar was in the shade of a nearby tree, standing on one leg, smiling happily, watching over us like a guardian angel.

Johannes was in his early thirties, lean and fit looking. He spoke English well with a wry, articulate turn of phrase. The boys and he had begun their walk at Vézelay in France, one of the traditional starting points, and had been on the Road to Santiago for over three months. They camped or slept in the open and usually cooked for themselves. To-night, as a treat, they had arranged to eat at the inn.

"Tell me about life in Northern Ireland." Johannes said it gently, as if with sympathy. It is a question often asked of those of us who live in that little corner of Europe. For years the media have illustrated our troubles with graphic accounts and pictures of the drama of violence. To those in other countries it must seem to be an impossible place to lead any kind of a normal life. It was a question that I had to try to answer.

I told him about the work in which I had been involved. To some it might have seemed of little importance when set against the politics of confrontation and violence. Johannes went back to carving the head.

"All over the world there is street violence, drug dealing, terrorism, famine, earthquakes . . .". As he was saying the words I knew that it was not meant as a counsel of woe but rather in understanding of the realities of life in modern times. I agreed.

"In Northern Ireland," I said, "We have our troubles but there are other countries where life is much more difficult. There is nowhere else I would rather have as home."

He asked me how I earned my living and I told him that I had voluntarily left an interesting job with the Sports Council in Northern Ireland after many years to work as a free-lance. It was to allow me to concentrate on projects which particularly interested me. He checked to make sure that he had heard me aright and then expressed himself amazed.

"I have uncles like you," he said "And they would never do such a thing." For a few moments he tapped the chisel to shave slivers of wood from the back of the head. "How can you leave a position of security and influence at your age?

He paused between the sentences expecting a response but I waited for him to continue.

"A free-lance has no security." he said and again I let him go on.

"Before, people had to listen because of your position but not now." He raised his head from his work and saw me smiling. "Forgive me." he said sheepishly, "I am too serious."

I told him that some of my friends had spoken to me just as severely. He laughed when I told him that one close friend had put it to me very bluntly.

"Bert Slader, Deputy Director of the Sports Council may be somebody in Northern Ireland to whom people will listen. Plain Bert Slader may not be anybody." Such risks are sometimes worth taking.

As we talked on I discovered that although he had good educational qualifications he had never had a permanent job. I tried to give him some idea of the work I hoped to do in the future through teaching, broadcasting and writing.

"Good" he said, smoothing the wooden head with his fingers. "If you make it work, it will be an interesting life." In a strange way it was a relief to find that this calm and relaxed young man now seemed to approve.

The boys had finished their work and stretched out in the shade, one to read, the other for a nap. I turned the questions on Johannes.

"Is one of the boys your brother?" I asked fancying I saw a resemblance.

"No" said Johannes and went back to his work.

Something prompted me to go on.

"Are they your friends?" Not wanting to seem too inquisitive I asked the question in as conversational a tone as I could manage.

"No." he said again, "No, not in the way you mean." There was a long pause and it seemed like the end of the conversation. After a few moments he set down his hammer and chisel and looked at me.

"I am their keeper." he said "Let me get you another cold beer."

When he came back he said something to the boys and they came over to join us.

"You look surprised" he said "But it is true. I am their keeper."

He explained that the boys had been convicted of offences in their own country and that the court had offered them, as an alternative to losing their liberty, the chance to walk to Santiago.

The deal involved them starting at Vézelay in France and spending five months on the Road. The rules were simple. They must not steal, or become drunk or break any of the laws of the country they were

conditioned and they arrived in the café looking cool and relaxed. But most of the car passengers came in looking tired, hot and at daggers drawn with each other.

One such family spent half an hour drinking great quantities of cool liquid, Coca Cola for the children and white wine for the parents. Gradually they began to feel better disposed towards each other and they left in good humour. As the door closed behind them it opened again and the senora came back to take another look at the mantecadas. She gave her order to the staff and fetched the rest of the family. Laden like a Maragata mule train, a dozen or more tins between them and driven by the senora as muleteer, they filed out, calling cheerfully to the bar staff and customers.

I drank sweet, white wine and tried the mantecadas. They were light, crisp and delicious. When the barman saw that I was enjoying them he brought me more.

"Eat for to-morrow." he said in Spanish, well aware that I was travelling on foot.

My bed-room over-looked the main road and after a short siesta I opened the shutters and sat at the window. As I watched, a group of people, men and women, boys and girls, in traditional costume, came out of a side street and entered the café opposite. They could only be Maragatos. I had read that occasionally they would wear traditional dress for a special event, perhaps a holy day or a fiesta. At the hotel reception I was told that there was to be a fiesta that evening in honour of San Pedro.

After dinner I followed the loud speaker music and found the fiesta about to begin in a small square a short distance away. The Maragatos were standing around in little groups, waiting for the festivities to start. I asked their permission to take photographs and they agreed with obvious pleasure, posing shyly for me and calling to their friends to come to join the group.

The men wore wide, black breeches with knee-high, felt boots, white shirts richly embroidered, black waistcoats worked in red, sashes and black felt hats like sombreros. The women's skirts and dresses were also black with a broad band embroidered in red and gold at the hem. They wore two shawls of gold and red, each in different shades. One covered the back of the head, the other was draped across the shoulders.

These striking costumes were worn with flair and familiarity as if the wearers were in their every day dress. How did they manage to show that they were graceful and proud and at the same time, shy and aloof?

The Maragatos trouped down the street to a plaza where a crowd had already gathered. At a signal they began to dance, slowly and gently, almost at walking pace. One of the men played both drum and fife, keeping the rhythm going with one hand and fingering the tune with the other.

The tempo changed and the dancers began to move more quickly, twisting and swinging in pairs. Like their easy familiarity with the traditional costumes, it seemed as if they had been moving in these patterns since they had learned to walk.

A part of the crowd now, I watched and listened with the local people in respectful silence. The dancers moved from tune to tune with grace and dexterity, enjoying the dance as dancers, not performers. And, although it presented a fascinating spectacle for the onlookers, I realised that these were movements which had evolved for those who were taking part, not those who were watching.

As simply as it had begun, the music ended and the dancers began to file away to the drummer's beat. The crowd was silent, there was no cheering, not even a tentative clap of appreciation.

I shouted "Bravo!" and felt embarrassed at the very idea of me doing such a thing. Encouraged by the daring of it, I shouted again, "Bravo! Bravo!" The crowd murmured approvingly and began to clap. Three of the older men in the dance troupe and the musician came over to where I was standing. They thanked me and took it in turns to shake my hand. One of them made a gesture towards the crowd and placed his hands, first over his ears and then over his eyes as if to say,

"They heard nothing and saw nothing." We smiled and I wished I could have told them that I recognised that silence. There are corners of the world where the local people find it hard to show praise or pleasure for their own. In Ireland they are called "the begrudgers", but that would have been too harsh a term for these people. They were, as their ancestors were reputed to have been, undemonstrative, shy, quiet to the point of dourness, but that need not mean that they were unappreciative.

The loud speakers began to boom with more modern sounds, mainly Latin American dance music and Spanish pop tunes. The throng grew and as the music became louder the atmosphere became more carefree and the people began to let their happiness show. The crowd confined itself to the pavement to leave the roadway clear for dancing but no one seemed to want to make the first move. Then, as the rhythm turned to the tango, one couple after another took to the roadway. They danced with such easy grace that although these dances are associated with South America, I realised that their style and form clearly originated in this country.

Others were slow to join in but when they did it showed how easily people of all ages can enjoy themselves together. A woman danced with

The Maragatos Dancers.

a baby in her arms. A teenager in denims had, as his partner for the rumba, an elderly lady, and they swayed and stepped in serious concentration and perfect time. Soon the roadway was full of couples of all ages and standards of dancing expertise. Women danced with other women if there were no suitable men to ask and a space cleared to allow a man to show off his six-year old partner as if she were a grand lady at the ball.

I stood amongst the watchers and shared the happiness. Unlike some of the earlier fiestas there was no sign that the consumption of wine had ensured the gaiety of this event. These quiet people were now allowing their natural good spirits and sense of fun to rule the evening.

Near me a girl noticed the stranger and smiled. She had dark hair and almond eyes. For a moment I thought she might invite me to dance, as if on her home ground it was up to her. She and her mother were standing at the front of the crowd, a little apart from the others, enjoying the fun but proud and reserved, keeping themselves to themselves. She turned her head and smiled again but there was no invitation to dance.

I remembered Walter Starkie's story of how he had been diverted on one of his pilgrimages. He had set out from Paris with three companions, two were French and one Basque. They followed the great Roman road to Chinon and found the town prepared for celebrations in honour of Rabelais. Of all the festivals that a pilgrim might happen upon on the course of his journey surely this must have been the least appropriate.

Rabelais, who of course gave his name to a style of bawdy, riotous humour, was born in Chinon in the 15th century. He was a friar, a priest and a doctor of medicine who focused his satirical wit on monks, priests and lawyers. He mocked contemporary learning and religion and in the most famous of his books left us such thoughts as " The appetite grows by eating". At least I had proved on this journey that the reverse of that was also true. In the same book he also gave the classic advice, "Do what you like."

Walter Starkie was a scholar and would have been familiar with the works of Rabelais. I could not, however, imagine him joining, on other than a very temporary basis, one of the groups of revellers he met on his visit to Chinon, "Les Compangons de Rabelais."

Becoming involved in the festival, Starkie hints at a series of temptations provided by, the "wine of one ear" and the intriguing "evil eye of Sybil of Panzoust". Between them they managed to lead him away from the Pilgrimage to Santiago to follow the Rabelaisian Road. Starkie decided that the telling in full of this story would have to wait until he had paid his debt to St. James by reaching Santiago on another occasion.

The following year he set out from Arles in the South of France to avoid the perils of the Rabelaisian Road.

But who was Sybil of Panzoust? I knew that the name Sybil was often taken, in medieval times, by women prophets who foretold the coming of Christ.

And what was the significance of her evil eye? If Walter Starkie did eventually tell the full story I have yet to read it. That evening in Astorga there was no sign of Sybil of Panzoust, and the look in the almond eyes was as innocent and friendly as Sybil's may have been evil.

At mid-night the fiesta was still in full swing. I needed an early start and turned away from the crowd to walk back to the hotel. A few of the Maragatos were eating rolls and cheese at a stall, still in their traditional costumes. One of the young girls hopped to one side and turned to swirl her skirts. Some modern clothes as worn by teenagers of her age seem designed to encourage a most ungainly slouching posture. This girl's clothes and movements were easy, graceful partners.

The group moved off in front of me along the street and the men, in their knee-high boots, stepped as lightly and easily as their forefathers, the muleteers, would have done as they crossed the rugged mountain country centuries ago.

I could only hope that, come the morning, I might tread so easily across the Monte Irago.

CHAPTER 12

The Wild Dogs of Foncebadon

Once in bed I could still hear the sounds of the fiesta on the warm night air, a pleasant lullaby easing me into sleep. At six-thirty in the morning I was up, dressed and packed. The bar was, of course, open for business.

Breakfast was coffee and mantecadas and as I ate, the sleepy waiter came over to my table with his hands raised in apology.

"A German gave me a message for the Irish pilgrim." he said slowly and hesitatingly in English. "He was here one day before and I was to say 'make a good trip'."

He paused and I nodded in understanding and thanked him in Spanish. As he walked away he turned on his heel.

"His name was Bruno." he said smiling. I imagined Bruno at the inn on the other side of the mountains wondering if I had arrived in Astorga and whether I was about to start for Foncebadon. The waiter came back to my table with a box of mantecadas as a gift.

"For the Camino." he said and we shook hands.

I left the hotel in good spirits, sorry to have missed Bruno but pleased to be setting out on this formidable stage on my own.

A pleasant country road led me out of Astorga and on the sky-line, over twenty-five kilometres away, was the crest of the range. There were patches of snow near the summits and the ridge looked a very long way in the distance. In a thicket I found a broken branch and fashioned myself a pilgrim's staff, neither as long nor as heavy as would have been traditional but straight and strong enough for my purposes.

The old route left the surfaced road, skirted the first of the habitations and came back to join the road at the small village of Murias. At this very early hour there were no people about but there were dogs and I was glad to be armed with the stout stick.

In most settlements where strangers might be expected, the dogs would be tied up or locked in behind iron gates. Some of them might snarl fiercely, or bark, or howl unhappily but they would be unable to attack the traveller. In more remote villages the dogs were usually on the loose. They would know the residents and, I assumed, the regular visitors, but strangers were a different matter.

At Murias the first dog loped towards me, barking loudly. I bent down pretending to pick up a stone and it stopped in its tracks. The barking had alerted all the other dogs in the village and they assembled as a pack, barring my way.

To my relief I spotted a faded yellow arrow on a wall, showing that the Camino left the road and followed a narrow lane which seemed to skirt the village. I smirked at the dogs and set off along the lane only to find, after a short distance, that a new pipe was being laid and the lane had become a deep water-filled trench. I tried walking on the top of the wall at one side of the lane but it was so unstable that there was a very real possibility of it and me collapsing into the trench. The brilliant tactical evasion had become a rout and I retreated to the road.

The dogs were waiting. No wonder they had not thought it necessary to follow me up the lane. I had the distinct feeling that local knowledge was enabling them to out-manoeuvre me.

The pack was now under the leadership of a huge off-white mongrel whose ancestors, presumably, had been usefully employed defending the village and its flocks from marauding wolves. The other members of the pack were of a variety of sizes and breeds with the smallest making the most noise.

They were out of luck. The difficulties in the lane had roused me from the quiet reverie of the early morning walk and the teetering moment on the wall had caused the adrenalin to flow.

I approached the dogs with menace, brandishing the stick and skittering a stone along the road towards them. They retreated a little and I roared at them like an angry cattle drover, swishing the staff through the air to let them hear its sound. The big mongrel slunk to one side of the road and the others followed, keeping him between themselves and me.

Once I had drawn level I slowed down, so that, as I walked away from them, it would not look like fleeing. This was the most difficult moment. Now that I was past them the instinct was to run but that would only have produced a chase which this pack of hounds were sure to win. Two or three times I stopped to turn and glare at them but by now they had decided to let me go.

The morning began to become warmer and I seemed to be covering the ground quickly. After three or four hours I had reached the foothills and the path climbed steeply. Soon I was amongst the mountains, high enough to look back and see Astorga through the haze.

The track turned another corner and there was a dramatic view of peaks surrounding a valley which fell away to the south. The Camino

curved to the north around the head of the valley and met the little road
that served the high villages. Almost immediately the route left the road
for a laneway and at the head of another rise entered the village of
Rabanal del Camino.

The houses were old, built of cut stone and timber. Usually the first
floor overhung the ground floor and the roofs were steep and slated with
large, heavy slates, fashioned to withstand hard, mountain winters. The
village was compact and picturesque and a little stream flowed down the
middle of its narrow street.

Two young girls dressed in woollen jumpers and tartan shirts were
playing and I asked them where I could find drinking water. They took
my waterbottles inside their house and returned with the kind of clear,
cold, fresh-tasting water that people in cities would pay good money to
be able to buy in bottles. The girls showed me the direction of the Camino
and wished me "Good-bye." in English.

The path crossed the open mountain. It was rough and so eroded by
the harsh weather of the hills that it was only possible to follow by picking
out the line of it well ahead. In a dip in the ground it met the road again
at Foncebadon and I could hear Bruno's pronunciation of it, Fon-cé-bad-
don, ringing in my ears. This was the village, recently deserted, which he
had warned me to avoid. He had advised keeping to the road which
passed around the settlement in a long northerly sweep on the easiest line
of ascent. I decided to ignore Bruno's counsel and left the road again to
see Foncebadon for myself.

The main street must once have been impressive. It was wide, paved
with cut stones and flanked by large houses, substantial dwellings for
such a remote mountain village. Now all was ruin and neglect. Grass and
weeds grew between the stones of the street. Doors swung creakily in the
light breeze. There were open windows with the remnants of curtains
still fluttering. Some roofs had fallen in, some house walls were partially
collapsed.

In the square a high cross of slender wooden spars looked as if it
would fall if touched. I imagined the Maragatos muleteers driving their
mule train up this street and hearing the stones ring when both they and
Foncebadon were in their heyday.

An abandoned village has an air which must touch the traveller's
spirit with melancholy. It is a sadness which regrets that all the life and
spirit that made and sustained the place are now gone. Unlike the ruins
of Greek temples or Crusader castles, monuments to an heroic and noble
past, the deserted village is a bleak reminder of the very temporary
nature of man's stay on earth. The line that came to mind was by Oliver
Goldsmith but not from "The Deserted Village". In his less well-known
poem, "The Traveller", he describes a river as:

The welcoming party at Rabanal del Camino.

"Remote, unfriended, melancholy, slow," and that line fitted Foncebadon.

The only sound, as I walked along the main street was the wind tugging at an open window or door and sounding hollow in the empty village. I was past the centre now and on my way out when suddenly there was a low growl close behind me.

The small hairs rose on the back of my neck and I turned to face a large dog, built like a Pyrenean, padding towards me. Behind it were three other dogs, two terriers and one a hound the size of an Alsatian. Compared with this pack, the dogs of Murias seemed like a bunch of household pets.

The Pyrenean growled loudly and nastily and the other three dogs joined in, barking furiously, advancing in line abreast. I still had the staff and some stones in my pocket from earlier in the day. I shouted and shook the stick but this pack was not as easily intimidated as the dogs of Murias. They barked and snarled more loudly and kept advancing in little rushes. I threw a stone at the Pyrenean, not to hit him but to clatter along the ground towards him. Trying for a direct hit on a moving target, it is very easy to miss. This way he would both hear and see the stone. It stopped him in his tracks for a moment.

I bowled a bigger stone to rattle down between them. To turn and move away at this stage would have been to invite attack, so I faced them, brandishing the stick and roaring abuse. Two more stones scuttling noisily turned the tide of confrontation in my favour. This was the effective weapon, they were afraid of stones. All four turned into a side street and in a few minutes I was out of Foncebadon and in open country.

I found myself laughing, probably in relief, but also at the weird and mock-heroic figure I must have cut in front of the poor dogs; this interloper in their village, waving a great stick, shouting in a language they could not be expected to understand but in a most menacing and unfriendly tone. However, no damage had been sustained by either side. Both parties had achieved their objectives, me to pass through the village, the dogs to retain squatters rights. Would that all conflicts might end so happily.

To have avoided the dogs I would have had to miss Foncebadon. For me, it had become a crucial link with the past and to walk through it was to feel the road as the pilgrims did. There are easier routes across the Monte Irago and quicker ways to travel but they would mean missing Murias, Rabanal del Camino and Foncebadon. For once I had not followed either Walter Starkie's or Bruno's advice but had the feeling, that had either been with me, he would have felt that we were on the right route.

The slower the journey the more impression each step makes.

At the head of the pass there was another cross. This one was tall and slender and its height was emphasised as it was set up on a huge mound of stones, boulders and rocks, carried to this spot by pilgrims and piled in a great untidy heap.

A short distance away was a tiny chapel built of stone and with its steep roof so constructed that it overhung the walls and provided shade. Two families had arrived before me. Their cars had been driven off the little road and across the rough terrain to be parked so close to the back wall of the chapel as to be almost touching it. This urge to drive cars designed for roads on to the open mountain is a phenomenon which I was well used to in Spain, but to find them here was still a surprise.

The men had lit a fire of dry brush wood in front of the chapel and closer to it than was safe. They were preparing to barbecue while their wives lay sun-bathing, stretched out in their bikinis like offerings to some pagan god of the sky.

At this height, with less atmosphere to beam through, the sun's rays are stronger and the heat and glare are intense. In the shade at one side of the building was a radio/tape machine of ghetto-blaster proportions. The music seemed loud enough to shake the little structure loose from its bed-rock foundations. I needed a rest and there was no other shade for miles so I walked over towards the chapel.

The men saw me coming but offered no greeting and turned away so they would not have to acknowledge mine. It was as if they resented the intrusion of anyone else into their corner of the wilds. Perhaps they thought that I might object to the lighting of the fire, or the loudness of the music, or the antics of their children, or the display of their wives so close to this place of worship.

If so, they need not have concerned themselves. It is a principle of survival that the mind concentrates on serious matters and ignores such minor problems and distractions.

I sat down on the stone bench at the other side of the chapel to attend to such important affairs as taking off my shoes and socks to let the burning feet feel the fresh air, to having a long rest in the shade, to slaking the thirst and quenching the pangs of hunger. I wiggled my toes and stretched them wide to let the air between them. I examined the sole of the foot with the blister wound and found the piece of Second Skin still firmly in place. I touched the wall of the chapel for luck and thanked The Three French Gentlemen yet again.

While the gas stove brought the water to the boil for coffee the young children came to watch and chat. They were as unsure of, as I was, of what was being said but we chatted quite happily as if this was usual. One of the women came to see what they were up to, smiled a greeting, and let them stay where they were.

The impact of the music was slightly lessened by the width and solidity of the building between me and the machine. It came in waves, pop, rock, traditional Spanish, English and Spanish pop, but the most frequent sound was that of American country and western music. As I ate my lunch I leant back against the wall and enjoyed it as I was enjoying the company of the children.

There were three toddlers and their curiosity was direct and un-selfconscious at the exact nature of each item of my food. Their parents had no need to worry that I might feed the children. There was no danger of that. I could hear the sounds of the feast being prepared and in such circumstances, where the receiver's need would be much less than his own, the traveller does not trade food for company. It might have been a different matter, however, had the deal been offered the other way around.

Well rested and refreshed I packed the rucksac, put on my socks and shoes with care and took a long drink of water from one of the bottles. It was time to go and, as I stepped from the shade into the searing heat, the barbecuing was at a crucial stage. The women were now helping but the principal difficulty seemed to be getting close enough to the fire to do the cooking without being grilled like the meat.

The young children watched me go with sad, serious faces. I waved to the cooks and some of them waved back. Behind me the guitars sang a country blues tune without words. In five minutes I was out of sight of the chapel and out of sound of the music. The mountain was still and calm and empty of people. I found it hard to convince myself that the picnic had been real and not a dream image reflected from some other occasion.

The afternoon was exceedingly hot and it was good to start feeling so cheerful with Molinaseca still twenty kilometres away. I reached the second pass and forced myself into a prickly bush to try to escape from the sun. It was an airless, uncomfortable seat and the hot rays filtered between the leaves.

I was across the main ridges, now it should be all downhill. The tiny village of Manjardin was deserted, there was not even a dog to bark at me. The name must have been a corruption of the French, "Mon Jardin", and another link with the French pilgrims who had travelled this route in such numbers. The houses of this hamlet called "My Garden" had been fitted together in a hillside hollow like dwellings in a Himalayan valley.

To the north there was a new symbol. On a hill the concrete and steel structure of a radar station now dominates the countryside.

The old route followed a long spur which led gently down into a deep valley. It was easy going but progress suddenly became more difficult as the yellow arrows directed me to a path which was almost overgrown with thorn bushes.

It is necessary to fight the vegetation in this kind of country. A machete would have been much more useful but I had my staff and I used it to whack my way through the thickets.

If the track had been used in the recent past, there was no sign of it. Paths like this need to be used if they are to stay open. Once the bushes begin to encroach, the foot traffic drops off quickly and nature claims back the territory.

I came out of the middle of a large bush to find myself on the edge of a village. It was a straggling, unkempt sort of place with ancient, wooden farm machinery leaning against walls, tangled with weeds. Somehow I found the main street. It was surfaced with sand and mud but there was a large patch washed clear by the rain, showing square-cut stones set together in careful patterns. It hinted that once, in another age, this had been a grand street.

Through the open door of one of the buildings I saw that the interior was a shop with a bar counter. There was no sign outside but this was the general store and it was stocked to bursting point with food, drink and merchandise.

I ordered an orange drink, a coffee and three hard boiled eggs from a glass case on the counter and sat down on a bench at a long wooden table. It was a pleasure to be sitting in the shade with a cool drink in my hand and, for the first time that day, I realised that I was very tired. The heat, the ascent and the distance were taking their toll but for a short while I could enjoy the delights of rest and refreshment.

Above my head were rows of smoked hams, so many that I wondered how the shopkeeper could keep track of them. I stood up and saw that each was carefully labelled. The information was written by hand and included a date. Over the counter, hanging from hooks in the ceiling, were paraffin lamps, galvanised iron buckets, Wellington boots, coils of rope and the same design of simple hand sheep shears as would be used on hill farms in Ireland.

The shelves were stocked with tinned food and the ends of the counter piled with clothes, trays of sweets and boxes of trinkets. The whole middle section of the bar counter was kept clear for action and the customers came in to lean against it and make their purchases. Behind it the shopkeeper was hard at work, arranging his wares, checking stock, making sales.

Some came only to chat and the man behind the counter kept an eye on me in case I might be bored. He spoke to me past his customers and, as far as I could make out from his words and gestures, he was describing them to me, usually in uncomplimentary fashion, sometimes even before they had left the shop. I gathered that one was mean, another could not count, a third did not know the difference between brandy and white rum.

As I left the shop the proprietor followed me out on to the street.

"Do not follow the yellow arrows." he said in Spanish and it took me a few moments to translate the words. I nodded and he continued,

"The path is bad, very bad. Walk to Molinaseca by the road." It was easy to take his advice. The road was free of traffic, shaded in parts and a most pleasant change after the struggle through the thickets.

The road met a river and on the other side was Molinaseca. A narrow and ancient stone bridge spanned the river and on a carved stone it was named as "The Pilgrims' Bridge." As I crossed it I asked a man about the inn and he shook his head.

"Cerrado." he said and seeing that I had obviously come a long way, he said it again sadly, "Cerrado." He was saying that it was closed and I tried to persuade myself that I had not understood the word correctly.

A little way along the street I asked another man and he confirmed the worst. The senora was ill and the inn was shut. He seemed concerned and brought me over to a group of women dressed in black. They formed a circle, in earnest discussion, occasionally glancing at me. Suddenly the meeting broke up and they were all smiles. "Senora Mercedez." the man said to me. Without knowing the magic significance of this name I thanked the women and the man guided me through the village.

The streets were narrow and clean, paved with cut stones. The first floors of the houses were overhanging and usually had a balcony guarded by a frail-looking iron rail. At a first glance the houses might have seemed in disrepair but I had passed through Rabanal and Foncebadon and Manjardin and had an idea now of what would stand the test of time.

When we reached the house of Senora Mercedez, she was out. Next door an elderly couple were sitting on a large stone carved as a seat. The woman rose and took charge. She told us that the senora was shopping in Pontferrada and would be back soon. She pushed her hand through a crack in the senora's door, opened it and stowed my rucksac in the ground floor room. It was whitewashed, stone-flagged, clean and tidy, everything in its place. Once the animals would have been stabled here and, in the winter, their heat would have kept the whole house warm. Now it was a hallway, a store and a workroom.

The woman locked the door after us and spoke to her husband who was still sitting on the stone. She gave him instructions loudly and in the tone which clearly indicated that she was used to being obeyed. He lifted himself wearily from his seat and gave her a look of dumb insolence.

"Come to the bar." he said to me. "We will drink wine and wait for the senora to return." I knew now what his wife had said and it was not what

Molinaseca Village.

he had been told to do that was annoying him but rather the manner in which he had been instructed.

He led me through a maze of narrow streets to where the village was connected to the road across the river by a bridge wide enough for vehicles. There was a café and in one corner a group of men and boys were arranging chairs around the television set as if a programme of some importance was due to begin.

The old man and I sat at a table near the bar. He nodded towards the group

"Football." he said indulgently "Bilbao and Athletico Madrid. If Madrid lose they will be happy."

I was surprised to find how easily I could understand his slow, slightly mumbled speech. He sipped his wine and began to grumble about his wife.

"She speaks to me like a mule." he said, "Come here! Go there! Do this work!" He was pleased to have someone to grouse to without being found out.

"I am seventy-six." he continued, "I am too old to be a mule."

I smiled sympathetically and now he had the grumble off his chest we began a long conversation based on simple questions and answers. He asked how old I was, if I was married, how many children I had, how far I had walked. I asked him about the village, his work and the radar station. We were on our third glass of wine when I broached the subject of Senora Mercedez.

"She is like my wife." he said cryptically, "All the women in this village are like my wife."

I knew that it was not meant to be complimentary but I had seen his wife in action and had been impressed by how decisively and quickly she had taken charge in the absence of Senora Mercedez.

We sat back on the wooden chairs and I felt happy and at ease. I was at a stage of tiredness when such a seat seems perfect comfort. My shoulders and back were relaxed, my legs and feet content to be still. After a long hard day's journey by car or coach, the traveller feels a great need to freshen up before enjoying relaxation and refreshment. Here I could sit, dust on my clothes and dried sweat on my brow, resting in the company of this grand old man. There was no hurry, the washing could wait.

My companion gave me a knowing dig in the ribs.

"You travel alone." he said and began to laugh. "My wife would not let me travel alone." he held his stomach as he laughed louder. "I am seventy-six and she would not let me away for one day." He shook with glee at the idea of it. "She knows," he continued when he was able to do so, "That I might not come back."

By this stage the football match was in full action. The fans around the television set shouted encouragement and the barman eyed them with amused tolerance. They were spending no money in the bar but they were local and were here as if by right.

The door of the café opened and standing in the threshold, against the bright evening light, was a sturdily built lady of medium height. She made an entrance.

"Where is my guest?" she said it loudly, in a tone which meant that she could be heard quite easily above the noise of the football commentary and the din of the fans around the set.

She spotted the stranger without difficulty and as we introduced ourselves the old man slipped away. The senora was clearly impressed that I had walked from Astorga and she questioned me about where I was from and where I was bound. She asked if I would like to shower before eating. Obviously I was now under her care and protection.

Having called the proprietor to our table, the senora explained that she had eaten in Pontferrada earlier and would not be cooking that evening. She told him that, sometime later, I would return to his restaurant for a meal. He looked pleased to have the booking. She wagged a finger in his face and, although I found it hard to make out what was being said, I gathered that she was giving him instructions. He was to treat her guest well. I might be leaving in the morning but she would still be here in Molinaseca.

I followed her through the door and she stopped with four women who were sitting on a low wall enjoying the evening sunshine. The senora knew an audience when she saw one. I had to wait while she explained to them that I was a pilgrim from Ireland who was walking from France to Santiago.

She took her time and it seemed a longer tale than I had told her. I stood patiently, having no option but to do so. Three of the women were impressed and nodded approvingly in my direction. The fourth was a tall, powerfully-built lady with carefully coiffured copper-blonde hair. She shook her head in disbelief.

"He is no pilgrim." I understood her to say, "He does not look like a pilgrim."

I laughed and she was not amused. Senora Mercedez ignored her doubts.

"To-day he has walked from Astorga" she said.

The tall woman said something which I could not follow but when she waved her thumb like a hitch-hiker I understood well enough. Senora Mercedez smiled knowingly, first at the three other women, then at me.

"She knows nothing." she said, dismissing the tall woman with an airy wave of her hand and a toss of the head. The other women smiled in agreement.

We walked slowly back to the señora's house and she acknowledged the greetings from her acquaintances in the village. The elderly couple were back on their seat on the stone outside their house. I thanked them for their help and they both looked at me like old friends. The senora preceded me up the stone steps at the back of the downstairs room.

At the top she opened the door of her living room. It was bright and spotlessly clean, neat and well ordered. She slipped out of her shoes and stepped on to two pieces of felt. The floor covering was linoleum, square patterned in shades of brown and cream. It gleamed with loving polishing. The senora slid across the floor like a dancer in an ice ballet and opened a door in the opposite corner of the room.

I looked down at my dusty trainers and decided not to incur her wrath. I had faced the dogs of Foncebadon but this was a different league. I slipped off my shoes and slid across the lino in my socks. The senora turned and caught me in the act. She was hugely embarrassed and I had to stand there in my sock soles while she wagged her finger and scolded me. She made it clear that as the guest there was no need for me to do as she did. I thanked her for not having to take off my shoes to cross her floor. It seemed the only sensible thing to do.

The bedroom was small and comfortable. She indicated that I was to sit on the bed and look out through the window. The view was framed by nearby trees and houses but the skyline in the distance was the Monte Irago. I said its name and the pleasure the sight gave me delighted the senora.

"To-night you will sleep under the mountain." she said and left me to do my unpacking.

Two minutes later she was knocking at my door to show me the shower. The bathroom, like the bedrooms and the kitchen, led directly off the living room and she showed me the facilities with pride. At first the gas geyser resisted her efforts to light it but quickly changed its mind when she hit it two sharp blows with the heel of her fist.

I stood under the shower, in the luxury of its gently warm stream of water and let the dust, grime and sweat be washed away. It took time but again, there was no hurry. While I was still under the shower I rinsed out a shirt, a pair of socks and a pair of underpants. They would dry overnight and during the next day and would be ready to wear that evening.

Travelling like this requires only one change of each of these items with light trousers as an alternative to the shorts I wore during the day, a sweater, a spare pair of trainers, a light water-proof and a hat to keep off the sun.

The Watchtower and glazed balconies at Ponferrada.

Towards the end of the 12th century the Order had become so powerful that the Knights were regarded as being a law on to themselves. They seemed too strong now to be disciplined by kings, too arrogant, too proud, too interested in power.

The church authorities, who had praised their work and held up their Christian values as an example to all, began to voice their concern. But the Order was now well established, its houses were substantial bastions, its wealth legendary. For another hundred years the Templars thrived.

At the beginning of the 14th century King Philippe of France, Philip the Fair, decided that it was time to attack the Order. He owed them money, he coveted their wealth and power. Being aware of their military skill and efficiency, he needed an ally and to gain an ally he needed an excuse.

His excuse was heresy. Philip's candidate for the vacant papal throne was the Archbishop of Bordeaux and, when he was duly elected and became Pope Clement the Fifth, Philip had the ally.

The Order of the Knights Templar was investigated by the Inquisition, charged and when found guilty, dissolved in a fury of torture, hanging and burning at the stake. By 1314 the knights in France were dead or dispersed in disgrace and the Order's treasures and land taken over by the Pope and the King.

Efforts to suppress the Order elsewhere were somewhat less successful. In Spain a few of the knights escaped capture and were able to elude their persecuters by becoming members of other Orders.

The castle at Pontferrada is a huge, battlemented, turreted pile of stone fitted together with such formidable intent that it might have remained here, unbreached, for a thousand years. It was the last redoubt of the Templars in Spain.

When the Templars were dispersed another order, the Knights of Santiago, took over the crucial role as Protectors of the Road in this area. Their power and wealth developed and they became one of the most formidable forces in the whole of Spain.

A famous, or perhaps more accurately, an infamous story of the Knights of Santiago was set on the other side of Astorga at the river Orbigo. It concerned a certain Suero de Quinones who claimed to be the champion knight of the Road to Santiago.

Foreign knights approaching the bridge from either direction were challenged to acknowledge that Suero's lady was the fairest of them all. In the summer of 1434 hundreds of jousts took place as he and nine other Spanish knights tested all comers. During thirty days of jousting there was a carnival atmosphere with music and feasting. The fame of Quinones, the Knight of Santiago spread; no longer the protector of pilgrims on the Camino, now merely the celebrated champion of ritual battle.

Like the Templars, the power and influence of the Santiago Knights made them a threat. The King and Queen of Spain, Ferdinand and Isabella, decided that the Order had served its purpose and should be dissolved. This time the deed was done with cunning and stealth. The Queen had her husband elected head of the Order and from this position Ferdinand quietly dismantled the entire organisation until only the title remained as a mark of distinction for noblemen.

Less than fifty years after Suero de Quinones had strutted so defiantly on the bridge over the Orbigo his Order was no longer a power in the land. Along the route, however, monuments remain, like the magnificent Monasterio de San Marcos in Leon.

As I entered the silent, empty dining room of the hotel I thought it might be yet another evening when I would be dining on my own. It was a well-appointed room and the tables, with their fresh white cloths and napkins, were laid in style with silver and glass. One table had a single deep red flower in a fine, narrow, cut-glass vase and I wandered over to look. The proprietor entered, smiled, and showed me to a place at the other side of the room. The door of the room burst open and a young man interrupted saying that he was in a hurry and asking to be served immediately. The proprietor showed him to a table and took his order.

My fellow diner emptied the contents of a briefcase on the table; maps, guide books, travel brochures and a large note-book took their allotted places before him. He was obviously a busy tourist, anxious to have the eating over so that he could be out and about his sight seeing again. He was in his early twenties, small and dark haired, dressed in casual clothes. He muttered fussily, shrugging at the litter of information and traced a route on the map with his finger.

His chair shot back and he leapt to his feet speaking the word "teléfono" to himself. He was running as he left the room, presumably to use the telephone. While he was out the proprietor came in with a tureen of soup for him, shrugged at the empty table and took the soup back into the kitchen.

An elderly lady entered, elegantly dressed in black and white, hair newly coiffured by a professional, walking with the aid of a stick. The flower had to be for her and she headed for its table with a murmur of appreciation. Having sat down with care, she hooked her stick over the back of a chair and she and the flower looked at each other in mutual admiration. She reached out and touched it gently with the tip of one finger and turned to acknowledge me with a gentle nod of her head.

"Buenos tardes senora." I said, trying my best to get the intonation right.

Assuming that a foreigner here must be French she replied in that language.

"Bon soir monsieur, et bon appetit." She spoke the language so naturally she might have been French but I was sure she was not. Her appearance and bearing were Spanish, in the style of a lady of substance. It was an easy guess that she was living alone, quietly and well, making the most of her circumstances.

The young tourist returned and our soup course arrived on the same tray, three china tureens in a row. The elderly senora helped herself to a little and ate with serious concentration. The young tourist filled his bowl and rustled his papers as he gulped his soup. I had chosen gazpacho, a chilled, vegetable soup of many versions, with tomatoes and garlic as the main ingredients, served with separate dishes of cubes of bread and chopped egg. Bruno would have approved of this cool, refreshing start to the meal.

Next I had a French omelette, delicately and aromatically flavoured with herbs, so freshly made it was still sizzling as it was served.

Two other customers arrived as we ate. One was a beautiful young woman, well dressed in high-fashion, casual style with her baby in a cot on wheels. She hardly noticed the attention of the proprietor as he showed her to a table beside the senora and seemed unaware that there was anyone else in the room. Her preoccupation was not on account of the baby which was sound asleep. She was lost in her own thoughts, her face drawn and sad.

The other was a young man, slim and above medium height. I had seen him earlier in the day dressed in a smart, tailored business suit. Now he was in his leisure wear and equally stylish. He was obviously a regular from the way in which he was greeted and he moved to his table with the grace of a professional dancer. It was his face, however, which was unforgettable. It was small and twisted to one side as if pulled out of true by an accident at birth. His bearing was that of a gentleman as he greeted the senora with charm and then spoke to each of the rest of us in the room.

The young tourist jumped from his chair to make another telephone call but no one seemed to notice. The baby wakened and made little squeaking noises as it stirred. The elderly senora leaned towards the child.

"¿Qué? ¿Qué va?". "What's wrong?" she was asking in quiet understanding of the ways of those so young. The mother's face relaxed for a moment and she smiled.

The main course was tender lamb in a thin sauce which smelt of herbs. It was accompanied by small, new potatoes and a salad. The young tourist rose from the table almost as soon as his was served and left. As far as I could make out he was telling the proprietor that he had no more time to waste. When he was gone, it felt as if some tension had eased in the room.

I sipped the wine and finished the meal with fresh peaches and a cheese made from goat's milk. The inns along the Camino were doing me proud.

The young mother left with her child and a few moments later the senora followed. She rose very slowly and leant heavily on her stick as she walked. The vibrant atmosphere in the room left with her. The young man with the twisted face was next to go and he smiled warmly as he wished me well.

The room had lost its lonely people.

Although I too was on my own and had no conversation with them, there was no feeling of loneliness for me, not at this stage of the journey. Their company had been enough.

The next morning I discovered the true size of Pontferrada. It took a long time to reach the outskirts and it seemed as if I had been best placed where I was. Many of the towns and cities I had passed through had managed, with a great sense of architectural style, to site old and new buildings as if they belonged together. Leon was the outstanding example. There the ancient and the modern set each other off and it seemed as if the pilgrims on the Road to Santiago had played their part. In Pontferrada the past and present are virtually separated, and fortunately so, they would not make happy neighbours.

The day was over-cast, humid and stiflingly hot. Although the sun was hidden its rays made my cheeks burn. It was pleasing to be facing less than thirty kilometres to Villafranca del Berzio, and to be aware that the lack of energy which I felt did not make the walking more difficult.

As I rambled along I had a sudden realization of being a different shape. When I started my journey I had been in good condition, feeling fit and healthy. I had prepared as thoroughly, and over as many months, as I had done when training for a marathon run a few years previously. Now my body had changed. I was not taller but leaner, and this was perhaps the reason for feeling that it was taking less effort to cover the ground.

The day became hot and clammy, and the sky more threatening. Near Villafranca there was a loud crackle of thunder in the distance. A group of cherry pickers were loading their harvest of bright berries on a trailer at the side of the road. The cherries were red, pink and white, in great glossy bunches. They called and when I crossed the road to them, they filled my two hands to see me on my way. To my surprise even the white berries were ripe, stretched to bursting with juice. As I walked I ate them all.

At the entrance to Villafranca the thunder was much nearer and the first shower of rain swept in on the wind. The drops were so big they made the dust jump. After three and a half weeks on the Camino I had decided to spend a night at a Parador and I saw its sign as the thunder boomed nearer and the rain began to fall in earnest.

In the entrance hall I took off my rucksac and the rain streamed down outside. The male receptionist accepted the booking without turning a hair at the sight of a dishevelled travelling man wanting to stay in his grand hotel. To be fair, the green and white glint of an American Express Card may have reassured him. For once I was glad to be able to use a plastic card to pay for the accommodation as I expected the bill to be somewhat larger than I had become accustomed to.

By the time I had been shown to my room the storm was at its height. I stood at the open window and watched great lightning flashes split the sky. The thunder claps were almost simultaneous so the eye of the storm must have been directly overhead. The rain poured down, cascading off the roofs in great gushes of water and flooding the small courtyard below.

My room was so large, so well-appointed and luxurious that it seemed unnecessarily so when my needs were so simple. I showered and lay down on the bed to watch the electric drama through the open window.

The storm passed, the sun dried the ground and the air smelt fresh. I walked into the town and found it attractive and friendly. Sitting at a café table under the colonnades I watched a group of thirty or more young people walk into the town, returning from a camp in the hills. They had been away for a few days and now they were back in civilization.

They dumped their gear under the arcades, arguing and jostling, scrambling to get share of any last pieces of food produced from rucksacs. While they waited for their transport to arrive they bought and shared soft drinks and made fun of each other. They were almost continually on the move, slumping on the ground for a few seconds as if to rest, then leaping up in case they missed any of the fun.

Back at the Parador I was in a different world. There were more residents than there had been at any of the inns. They were well-dressed, obviously affluent and experienced travellers. In the dining room that evening they all seemed to be pilgrims on the way to Santiago, travelling quickly and in style, their cars poised in the car park for the next day's stage.

If I had met Bruno on the way into Villafranca I doubted that I would have been tempted to stay here, just one night in a Parador.

CHAPTER 14

O Cebrero: The Village in the Clouds

Villafranca del Berzio is at the bottom end of a narrow gorge where the river and the Road to Santiago are hemmed in by steep cliffs. It bears the name Valcarcel, the Prison Valley. The town is picturesque and has a impressive feature - well-preserved manorial houses with wrought iron balconies which are set on carved stone plinths or supported by ornate wrought iron stays.

The settlement was founded by foreign pilgrims in the 12th century around an important hospice. As the foreigners were known by the Spanish as Francos, the town became Villafranca. The Palace of the Dukes of Alba overlooks the town and has an air of grandeur and importance but the buildings in La Calle del Agua, or Water Street, are much more evocative of pilgrim times. This is an authentic part of the old route and still used as such. The houses are fronted by fine portals, ancient coats of arms and elegant iron work. There are hanging baskets of flowers in bloom, of such colour and profusion that the old street seems still in its heyday.

In the corner of a small square is the Hostal Commercio Puente Neuve. In Ireland there must be an establishment with the same name, the Newbridge Commercial Hotel. Here it is a building which looks so old that it seems most unlikely that it is still functioning as an accommodation for travellers. The inn yard is approached through an archway big enough to admit a coach and horses. The entrance hall is at the back and, as I passed, the door was open. However, the hostal is still very much in business and next time I visit Villafranca I know it will be to stay here.

As I left the town in the morning it was overcast and wet, and the walls of the Valcarcel were hung with damp mist.

General Sir John Moore and his army passed this way in the winter of 1808 in ignominious retreat, deserted by their Spanish allies, harried by the French, morale and discipline disintegrating. As the column slogged up the long slope to the Piedrafita Pass, such was their state of exhaustion that the soldiers pay had to be dumped. The starving men watched while the wooden barrels filled with gold coins were rolled down the mountainside. Women camp followers and soldiers died at the roadside, some in a drunken stupor on looted wine.

General Moore did his utmost to keep his men together hoping to reach the port of La Coruña and the British ships waiting to evacuate them. As his men were embarking, Moore was killed in a rearguard battle but eight thousand of his troops managed to escape. Amongst them was a hardened core who lived to fight another day under Wellington. They took part in the defeat of their French pursuers and then Napoleon himself.

For me it was a wet, miserable day in summer. For those desperate soldiers it was the very depths of a mountain winter.

Although the cloud enveloped the whole landscape in dense, damp mist it was a relief to leave the Prison Valley and cross the pass. The visibility was so limited that it was hard to find the village on the mountain crest and when I did, the sign had been changed from "El" to "O" Cebrero, the first hint that I had crossed into the Province of Galicia and that Castilian Spanish was no longer dominant.

The village was tiny, set low on the open hillside to withstand the weather. Some of the houses had thatched roofs, others were neatly slated, all were fitted into the slope rather than perched on it. Behind a wall was a small church built in the 9th or 10th century and attached to an inn added a few hundred years later, the famous Hospederia San Geraldo de Aurillac.

The inn is run by the sister of the village priest and her family. It is the very essence of the hospitality provided by such places along the route since medieval times. A stone flagged hall leads to a large room which acts as reception, dining and sitting room for all the customers. The table tops are scrubbed wood and for seats there are simple wooden chairs and benches. In one corner is a huge fireplace and, on the day I arrived, a fire of big logs made the room warm and cheerful.

I was shown upstairs to a bedroom as small as a monk's cell, recently panelled with pine, clean and comfortable. For the first time on the journey I felt ill. It was a queasy, sickening sensation in the digestive system which had been developing all day. I lay down on the bed and felt the tiredness of the whole journey. After a doze I stirred myself to rise on one elbow and look out through the window, set deeply in the thick wall. When Walter Starkie reached O Cebrero he discovered a wonderful, awe- inspiring view of peaks and valleys stretching as far as the eye could see. I saw only a wall of grey cloud close enough to touch and heavy rain settling on the hillside rather than falling. It was easier to imagine the passing of Moore's demoralised army than Starkie's elated visit.

Out of the mist a huge white Pyrenean dog lumbered lazily towards the back of the inn. It lay down on the rough grass and, in the streaming rain, proceeded to make itself comfortable. Its thick coat seemed to fluff out for maximum protection and was, of course, designed for survival in these conditions. For no logical reason he seemed a much more friendly animal than the Pyrenean that had led the pack in Foncebadon and I hoped I would have the chance to speak to him before I left.

I must have slept the early evening away for I was wakened with a jolt by a loud knocking on the door. It was the inn-keeper, shouting to me that dinner was finished. It was not, of course, it was her way of telling me that it soon would be if I did not present myself without delay.

The worst of the sickness seemed to have gone but I felt weak as I came downstairs. To my amazement the main room was full. There were long tables with parties of young people and a family and small groups of friends at other tables. The meal had obviously been in progress for some time and I squeezed myself into a corner place at a small table. It felt better to be amongst the hub-bub of noise and activity.

The young people at one of the long tables were Spanish teenagers in excited conversation, their leaders speaking loudly, trying to hold their attention. On the other side of the room was a smaller group, obviously French, keeping each other amused in noisy fashion. Two of the leaders watched and a third joined in the fun as rowdily as the rest. I gathered that both groups were not staying at the inn. The Spanish were camping and the French in residence in a barn. Near me the other guests were quietly absorbed in their own company but beginning to show signs of annoyance as the level of noise made by the young people rose.

At the other end of the room, beside the fire, was a large square table occupied by local people. The inn-keeper's brother, the priest, was there and I assumed that the others were family and friends. The group contained three or four generations and was calm and self-contained, totally separate from the others present. It seemed as if they had always been here in this room, like the open fire, a constant part of its life, while the travellers paused and then moved on.

I ate very little but enjoyed the meal. The Spanish group became even more intensely absorbed in their conversation. The French were now playing a simple game of cards, similar to Snap. As they played, apparently oblivious to everyone else in the room, the noise increased as the game progressed. It reached a crescendo as the final card was slapped down at the end of each round with a shout of glee. The leaders seemed unaware that the loudness had reached the point where the game was dominating all the other activity in the room.

The inn-keeper was in the kitchen, presumably attending to the chores. The younger members of her family who were serving ignored the noise but some of the Spanish group turned to glare at the rowdy card players.

Eventually one of the children at the priest's table was sent to the kitchen with a message. The inn-keeper's eldest daughter appeared in her apron. She was a tall, handsome, tousled-haired woman with a country-air complexion and a sense of fun. But for the present, flushed from the heat of her work, sleeves rolled to the elbow, she looked exceedingly formidable.

She approached the French group with intent and addressed them leaning with her hands on the table. They listened in silence and must have understood what was said for they paid the bill and left quickly. As they did so the leaders managed to look sheepish without acknowledging anyone in particular. The room was a different place without them, more comfortable but less alive.

The Spanish teenagers smirked and smugly installed themselves in front of the hearth, thereby isolating everyone else in the room from the fire. An elderly lady at the priest's table leaned towards them and had a quiet word. They retreated and the pattern of the evening settled itself like water in a pond reaching its natural level after a flurry of rain.

In the morning the cloud was still lying its full length on top of the village. The wind was pushing at the grey vapour, trying to shift it without success. I was not yet recovered but in good spirits, well enough to appreciate this unique mountain settlement and to feel I could continue.

O Cebrero seemed strangely familiar, as if I had been here in a previous life. Perhaps it was due to the Celtic feel of the village and its people, and the way the damp clouds touched the open hillside.

The thatched houses are called pallozas and are round or oval, with dry stone walls. It was obvious that some of the buildings had been recently renovated for the thatch was corn yellow, clean and neat. It was curved at one end and carefully secured against the wind. It is the sort of roof covering that requires to be well laid and regularly maintained. So done, it makes a house weatherproof and warm. In some parts of Ireland thatch only ceased to be used because the people were too poor or too parsimonious to have the job done by experts. They tried to do it themselves and some older people still have childhood memories of the buckets and pots set out to catch the drips in wet weather. A poor thatch looks dull and lifeless of itself and has grass and weeds growing through it. The impression is that one day soon it will collapse of its own accord. The roofs of O Cebrero were in no such danger.

The church has been in use since the very earliest days of the pilgrimage and became famous in the 14th century as the site of a miracle. It concerned a none-too-enthusiastic priest who was posted to the village to say mass for the pilgrims and local people. In a bad spell of winter weather few pilgrims came and the priest became reluctant to leave his warm fire and make the short journey to the church. One evening there was a snow storm and only his most regular attender, an old shepherd, was waiting for him to say mass. As he did so the priest muttered that only a fool would come out in such weather for a piece of bread, a drop of wine and a few words of Latin. There was a clap of thunder as he spoke and the bread and wine were transubstantiated. The story of the miracle was passed on by the pilgrims and soon known throughout Europe. The relics are preserved in caskets presented by Queen Isabella. The chalice used by the priest is Romanesque and, perhaps because of the presence of the Knights Templar in the area at the time, is reputed, by some, to be the Holy Grail.

The road was wet, misty and empty of traffic. I crossed the Puerto de Pyo pass and the old route left the surfaced road. It swept downwards, still in heavy cloud, on an easy track and felt, for it was not possible to see, that it was skirting the side of a steep valley. All of a sudden the clouds split and the sunshine flashed on scores of wild broom bushes in full bloom. The yellow flowers formed a head-high alley for me to walk through, as twice the cloud closed in and broke again to let me see the view.

Once it had cleared I sat down on a stone to make a cup of coffee and look at Galicia. Directly below were steep, green, wooded valleys and miles of peaks and ridges stretching towards the horizon's rim. It was easy to see now why others had been impressed by the view.

Travelling across the landscape from the Pyrenees I had seen the different faces of Northern Spain, but here in Galicia I might have entered another country.

Around a corner in the track came two teenage boys in a hurry, so absorbed in trying to out-speed each other that they missed my greeting. They were part of the French group who had eaten at the inn on the previous evening. Ten minutes later the others appeared, chatting loudly, and, like the first two, carrying nothing except a sweater or an anorak tied around the waist. I sat for a little while longer to let them get ahead and then followed through the beautiful broom.

The Camino took a natural line down a long curving ridge, passed through small villages and reached the valley of the Rio Sarria. I entered the village of Tricastela through a farm yard and on to the main street. At first glance it seemed that there might be little enough of interest in Tricastela. I knew that once it had been an important stopping place on the Pilgrim Road, providing accommodation for considerable numbers. There was also a pilgrims' jail with inscriptions carved by the inmates including the French symbol of liberty, the cock. Now the village looked quiet and slightly run-down as if its day was long past.

Bruno's list indicated that there was a restaurant which had rooms to let and I found it without difficulty. It was one of the few new buildings in the street and my room was spacious and comfortable. Next door was the bathroom and it was a revelation. It was bright and stylish, fitted and furnished in marble, glass, ceramic tiles and soft, tasteful fabrics. Aware that it must have cost a substantial sum, I wondered if there were grants to help provide tourist facilities. If so, the money had been well spent.

Cleaned at length in the luxurious bathroom and rested at leisure in the comfort of the bedroom I went out to explore the village at a gentle pace.

The French group had arrived and were sitting in the shade on seats provided at a bus stop. The leaders looked harassed and I walked over to pass the time of day. Although I was not able to find out where they had started, they had been on the Road to Santiago for many days. Their gear was being transported by mini-bus and they intended to spend the night near Tricastela. The two boys who had gone off in front were now missing and one of the leaders was searching the surrounding countryside in the mini-bus. This accounted for the worried looks and one explained that the two boys did not know that Tricastela was the end of that day's stage.

The other young people seemed tired but happy to have completed another section of the Camino. None of them had any idea of the route or where they were in relation to Santiago. Their leaders, who held such secrets, resigned themselves to waiting for the two lost pilgrims to turn up.

Beside a stretch of open ground, which probably acted as market place or village square when required, I found a café. Outside was a lopsided table whose top was a great, thick slab of slate balanced on a sturdy trestle. From this perfect vantage point I watched the village come to life in the early evening. Old friends met and took part in dramatic conversations which I wished I had been able to understand. Dogs chased each other around the square and the nearby farm buildings.

A boy came with news that a broody hen had hatched her chicks in a hedge across the road. The barman's wife took charge, it seemed it was her hen. The fowl was so well ensconced in the thicket that she and half a dozen young helpers failed to dislodge it.

A man was required and her husband appeared. He fought his way into the middle of the prickly bushes and, after a deal of struggling and crying out in pain, presumably caused by both hedge and hen, he emerged with a fine brood of chicks in a cardboard box. While the chicks were being shown to me and the small crowd of interested spectators, the woman chased the hen around the square and finally cornered it in an outhouse. There was a round of applause and well-merited congratulations and, being a customer, I was as pleased at their success as they were.

Leaving Tricastela next morning through a narrow muddy lane I was aware of a special feeling of affinity to this unprepossessing place. Behind the main street the buildings looked dilapidated. There were wooden farm implements leaning against walls and a single shafted bullock cart with a wooden axle and solid wooden wheels.

This village has been on the route of the Camino since the 10th century. In the Codex Calixtinus it was mentioned as the place where pilgrims should pick up a stone and carry it to Santiago to make lime for the Apostle's Basilica. It lacked the picturesque charm of many of the other villages on the route but I was in no doubt about my own response. In one short evening I had enjoyed its friendliness and felt the rhythm of its life.

I was travelling to the beat of the same drummer.

CHAPTER 15

The Lanes of Enchantment

The hills were covered in mist as the path wound through leafy, muddy lanes and climbed steeply out of the valley of the Rio Sarria. At a high point above Tricastela the mist cleared and revealed a wonderful view. The valley was deep, with wooded slopes and, twisting away to the south-west were ridges of rugged hills, range behind range.

On higher ground the feeling was again familiar. The track rose across the open mountain and was bordered by heather, ferns, brambles and the glorious broom. It could have been on the side of a sheltered glen in Scotland or Ireland. The difference was that here it was warmer, much warmer. As the day became hot the mist closed in again and, through a stable yard, I entered the first of a succession of tiny villages. In each I asked for the name of the village.

"¿Cómo se llama esto pueblo?" and repeated the name when told, so that the person I had asked could correct my pronunciation. I even asked the question when I knew the answer.

Trying to relate the route on the ground to the large scale map presented some difficulty. The track seemed to twist and turn its way through the hills but the map showed that it was a fairly direct line. In this type of country traditional routes run with the grain and not across it. They respect the shape of the land.

The little villages were a delight. Every few kilometres I would happen upon one and it provided shade, cool, clean water and a moment or two of company with its inhabitants. These hill settlements are not connected by a surfaced road to each other or the outside world. Their links are tracks which have been used, very much as they are now, by people, farm animals and carts over the centuries.

At irregular intervals there are small pilgrim shrines often hung with freshly cut flowers, and occasional tiny chapels, some well cared for, others neglected and crumbling away.

There is no need, however, to preserve the old route over these hills, it still provides the way for local travel. The tiny villages are strung together by the Road to Santiago like unmatched, rare stones on a necklace.

The mist, which had been closing in and clearing since early morning, finally dispersed in the heat of the afternoon. The track led into a farm yard and passed through an ancient building under a huge, slated archway into the village of Pintin. I discovered the name by asking and it was one of the few settlements whose name corresponded to that given on the map.

Through a doorway, like a low hole in the wall, I entered a small room which was both shop and bar. There was no sign outside, but a few crates of empty bottles and a pile of cardboard boxes were sufficient clues. I sat down on a rickety chair and ordered a bottle of orange. There was no refrigerator and thus no point asking for a cold drink. All the stock was in this one room and on display. The space was tiny and the goods were in little groups on shelves and on the floor. The range was small and there were few items of stock in each line but everything was to hand.

A commercial traveller was standing at the counter, note-book at the ready. He was thin, dark haired, pale, and courteously moved to one side when I entered so that the shopkeeper might make a sale. Now he was back persuading his client to buy. It seemed like hard work. At a very gentle pace he was going through his list, item by item, in that patient helpful way which all good commercial travellers have acquired.

The shopkeeper was a larger, bulkier man, of weathered complexion, probably middle-aged but looking older. He was dressed in a way which showed that he had lost interest half way through the process. His look was sad, slightly woebegone, as if the business of buying was proving worrisome.

Each time the salesman mentioned an item the shopkeeper frowned and rubbed his chin. He considered carefully and only ordered with reluctance. They came to the drinks section of the list and the salesman mentioned Coca Cola. The shopkeeper shrugged and nodded at the case and a half in the corner. The salesman pressed on and I was surprised to hear him get orders for some of the liqueurs. It was only for single bottles but it showed that there must be a demand for fine drinks in Pintin. The shopkeeper brightened up when they came to brandy. He was down to a bottle and a half on the shelf and cheerfully ordered three more.

I remembered the late Thursday afternoons of my childhood. The traveller from the Belfast Co-operative called for the family grocery order just after I had arrived home from school. We bought milk, bread, coal, meat and clothing as well as groceries from the great range of shops and delivery services run by the Co. A number came to mind, 31299, our family number. When it was used to purchase an item, however small, a discount was credited to our central account with the company.

The grocery travellers from the Co-Op. were always the most cheerful and pleasant of men. They never pushed for a big order. They knew their customers and what they could afford. They came into the homes as friends of the family. The commercial traveller in Pintin could have worked for the Co. in Belfast.

He packed his order book and went out to the car for those items he had brought with him. The shopkeeper examined each in turn, checking the seals on bottles and turning the tins and packets over in his hands looking for damage. The salesman smiled at me in embarrassment and helped stack the goods in the right places.

When he left the strain and worry faded from the shopkeeper's face and he busied himself happily with his new stock, carefully arranging and re-arranging where necessary. He smiled the faintest of smiles when I paid him and left the cool of his little shop.

Pintin was connected to the main road in the valley by a narrow quiet country road. It was hot walking but gently downhill and I strolled into the town of Sarria at the end of the afternoon.

For three days I had been passing through and stopping in villages.

O Cebrero perched on the top of the mountain pass, Tricastela in the valley, and the tiny remote hamlets which had made this day's journey so interesting. By contrast Sarria was a proper town, a busy commercial centre at important road and rail junctions.

I climbed steep steps to the older streets on a height above town. Looking back I saw two of the young people from the French group and this time they waved and shouted a greeting.

Sarria was once capital of this eastern corner of Galicia. Its location has given it a strategic position and its size, in relation to the surrounding villages, has made its presence significant in the area. Its importance on the Road to Santiago was firmly established in the 14th century when Pope John the 12th sent a Papal Bull from Avignon. Under the terms of this, indulgences were conceded to those in Sarria who assisted pilgrims by providing lodgings and alms or who administered sacraments to them.

Bruno's list of places to stay named three in the town. The first noted was a fonda but it proved elusive. I tramped the streets asking and searching without result and then a man directed me to a bar of the same name. It was a small, new establishment, fitted out in contemporary style and lively, even at this time of the day. The owner nodded when I asked about a room and indicated that I should follow him. We walked down the street a little way and entered a building in a nondescript row.

It had been constructed fairly recently and then allowed to deteriorate rapidly. An open stairway, in a dirty grey hall ankle deep in litter, led to a locked door on the first floor. A small peeling sign announced that this was indeed the Fonda. We entered a landing where the paint work was scored, discoloured and flaking. The plaster beneath was crumbling away to leave holes in the surface of the wall and little piles of white dust on the floor. The building echoed as we walked and somewhere ahead a lavatory cistern hissed and gurgled.

The barman opened a flimsy door and, without enthusiasm, showed me into a bedroom. The decor was in a similar state to that of the landing. The window was star-cracked and dirty. There were tell-tale holes between the skirting board and the floor, although I found it hard to imagine why mice or rats would want to visit. Surely there must be much richer pickings elsewhere in the town.

My guide waited as I turned back the bed-clothes and the sheets looked relatively unmarked. Not as clean as might have been expected had they been changed since the last occupant, but not visibly dirty. It took a matter of moments to consider the position. I was thirsty and tired. It had taken quite a while to find this place. Maybe the other establishments on the list were worse. I need only be in the room to sleep. It was cheap. It seemed that I might have the entire fonda to myself.

"A pilgrim's needs are simple." I could hear Bruno's voice whispering in my ear. The decision was surprisingly easy, I agreed to take the room. The barman smiled for the first time, handed over the keys and left me to settle in.

It was a relief to change my shoes and socks. I put the shoes out on the window sill to air and steeped the socks in the cracked wash-hand-basin. There was one hook on the wall of my room and I hung some of my clothes on it and also the rucksac with everything else left unpacked, in the hope that any small four-footed intruders would not be able to jump high enough.

Nothing could disguise the fact that this was a seedy, dingy room but, now that I was installed, it had lost its awful look. The bed seemed reasonably comfortable and at least, I had a room for the night. I wondered whether the Papal Bull of 1332 still applied and, if so, whether the owner of this fonda would be eligible for its benefits.

In the early evening I climbed the hill to the older part of the town for the view. The group of Spanish teenagers I had seen at O Cebrero were taking off their rucksacs and preparing to enter a church. None of them gave any sign of recognition. It was not rudeness. They were tired, some were so foot-sore and weary they could hardly stand. As a group they were still completely self-absorbed, as they had been at the Hospederia.

As a contrast to the Fonda I ate in a smart restaurant, with a seat in the dining room which overlooked the river. The meal was good. The restaurant, and later the town itself, were pleasant places to spend an evening.

When I went back to my room it felt like a small furnished corner of a derelict building. As I lay down on the bed the bathroom along the corridor came to life. How is it possible for water moving along a pipe to do so with a dull tapping sound?

Of the two books I had brought with me one was now lost. It was The Quiet Mind, a tiny publication and thus very suitable for carrying on such a journey, but lost in the folds of a coverlet at the first inn.

I opened the one still with me, a thin, light, austerity version of Penguin's Selected Poems by T.S.Eliot. It was hard to imagine losing this slender volume. It had travelled with me since student days on journeys in Europe, Asia Minor, Iran, Afghanistan and on mountain peaks from the Arctic to the Himalayas. I opened its pages at The Love Song of J.Alfred Prufrock and found the line, another "...one-night cheap hotel".

The lavatory cistern joined the water pipe with a steady, noisy trickle, Its valve hissed and little lumps of water plopped into the bowl. Two taps were each making their own distinctive sound. I guessed that one must be a bath tap as it had the advantage of an echo chamber effect. In other circumstances this cacophany might have jarred on the nerves and prevented sleep. Here they played their parts like instruments in a work of modern serious music. In this unkempt room, in the dilapidated fonda, it was a lullaby and I slept well. If there were small visitors during the night, looking for crumbs of food, they came and went on tip-toe.

In the morning I climbed the hill again to the top of the town and left Sarria with a view of its Romanesque Church and castle ruins. The route wound, through leafy lanes wet with dew, to the crest of a low ridge. It was as if this idyllic section of the Camino was in compensation for the accommodation at the fonda. The previous few days had shown me the freshness of the Galician countryside. Here the Road to Santiago carried me along natural travelling lines through farmland, woods and hills. High hedges provided shade from the morning sun. By eleven the dew was gone and the early morning mud on my training shoes dried to dust and fell away as I walked.

These were the lanes of enchantment.

There were places where the route of the Camino is not needed for local travel between villages and farms and where the lack of use might have caused it to become overgrown. On these parts an effort has been made to cut back the ferns, the whin bushes and, that bane of travellers on foot, the all-pervading bramble. This simple work of clearing has revealed the surface of the old road, on one section set with cobbles and on another paved with large flat stones, laid with great skill and care in some distant age. By the efforts of some society of friends of the Camino the ancient surface is being preserved for use by the pilgrims of the present and the future. Further on, sand had been scooped from the bed of a stream to make a dry, silver trail beside the water.

One of the Lanes of Enchantment.

There were more pilgrim shrines, one an altar set beside the track as convenient as a wayside well. Its working surface was a large flat slab supported by two upright stones and backed by a tall slab with a figure carved in relief. Every pause for pilgrims must have been time for prayer and rededication.

The trees were in great clumps of natural woodland. The oaks and Spanish chestnuts created a special, atmospheric light, neither bright nor dark. It illuminated the glades in layers of brightness, graduated from ground to topmost branches and patches of sky. I saw the first of the eucalyptus trees, their slender trunks with peeling bark and no lower branches, reaching straight up towards the light. At their tops the leaves flickered silver and grey and, here in the open air, the powerful scent of eucalyptus was a gently pervading aroma.

The valley of the Rio Miño was dramatically revealed as the track wound through trees and came out on the open hillside with the river far below. It was an impressive valley, deep and wide amongst the hills. The bridge leading to the small town of Portomarin was directly below but still a long way away.

Two hours later, at the end of the afternoon, I stepped on to the bridge.

There were small pleasure boats in the water and a bank was laid out like a beach with picnicking families, sun umbrellas, sun bathers, sellers of cold drinks and snacks. The cars were, of course, parked as close as possible with bonnets and boot lids open to let the air circulate around hot engines and to give easy access to the food and fun equipment. I remembered that it was a Saturday. The local people were on holiday and had come to the water for the day.

This is the River Miño which flows through Galicia to the Portuguese frontier and there becomes the famous Rio Minho. Here it has been dammed to provide a water supply and has filled a part of the valley where once the old town of Portomarin served the pilgrims. The original bridge had been built to facilitate the pilgrims and the town had grown around it on both sides of the river. The new bridge strides the four hundred metres across the new width of the water and Portomarin has been rebuilt on a height above.

The original fortress church was built by the Knights of St.John of Jerusalem and, before the reservoir came into service, the building was taken down stone by stone and re-erected as part of the new town on the hill above.

I walked up the steep road away from the excitement and bustle of the Playa Miño to the recreated Portomarin. The new settlement is calm and arcaded, glistening white in the sunshine, muted with old stone work. It looks much older than its years, the lay-out of the streets and the style of the buildings being of the distant past.

Fortified 12th century church at Portomarin.

The fortress church stands four-square and solid, the numbers on its stones evidence of its painstaking re-location. The original site was chosen by the Knights as a strategic location. Now it overlooks the main square, a part of the town rather than its dominant feature.

The only busy place was the inn, the Postada del Camino, its bar full and its customers spilling out on to the terrace. There was every sign of it having had a hard day's business. The young man who was in charge looked exhausted. He led the way to the dining room where, although the customers had long since gone, the tables were still piled with the debris of lunch.

I followed him through the pokey kitchen and up a narrow flight of stairs to the bedrooms. Mine was small and basic but well above the class of the previous night. I unpacked and showered at leisure and strolled out to explore the town before the evening meal.

It was still warm and I sat on the steps of a colonnaded building near the church to enjoy the fresh evening air and the day's heat in the stones of the steps. They combined to ease the body and relax the mind. I leaned back against a pillar to look at the fortress church.

There was one large, beautiful rose window set high on the front wall. The arch and doorway were Romanesque and set tight in a wall built to withstand the batterings of war. That such an obvious fortification could also be a church was an architectural conjuring trick. It could appear as either or both depending on where the eyes rested. The figures carved above the door had been damaged, not by weathering or accident, but deliberately defaced, another mark of conflict.

Directly opposite the church is a colonnaded building in traditional style. A door opened at the front to reveal that the interior was a sports hall. Behind the ancient facade was a modern construction which reverberated to the crash of ball on woodwork and the squeal of training shoe on non-slip floor. Someone pulled the door closed to keep the ball in play and shut the noise in too. The square became quiet and empty again.

At this stage of the journey it was easy to sit in such a place and to wait, without the slightest impatience, for something to happen. It did.

Around the corner of the church came two teenagers, slouching with long, slow, ungainly strides. They shouted across the square obviously in recognition. For a moment I wondered why. Then I realised that, in unwitting disguise, it was the two boys from the French group who had greeted me in friendly fashion in Sarria.

Then they had been dressed in shorts, Tee-shirts and trainers but that had been for walking. Now they were in their finery. One wore jeans and a stunning, multi-coloured sweat shirt and he sat down on the steps, content to listen. The other stood in front of us ready for a chat. He was wearing black boots with heavy, studded soles, black puttees, black and white candy striped trousers. He had a leather waist-coat studded with metal rivets and festooned with chains, a massive chain belt and wire loop ear rings.

"Where did you get the gear?" I asked him in his own language, hardly able to believe my eyes and in admiration at this total transformation.

He was not prepared for the tone of appreciation and for a moment he looked shy. Then his confidence returned in a rush of words.

"It is my own." he said proudly in French. "It travels in the mini-bus."

Now that his style had been shown off he crouched, to come down to my sitting level, squatting like an Indian brave.

We talked in a mixture of French and English helping each other with the words. His group was staying in Portomarin for two days or more so that some friends could join them for the last stages. We admired the church and talked about our two very different journeys on the same road. His companion said little but was part of the conversation.

They wanted to find out what I thought about Spanish food but hesitated, finding it hard to ask the question without sounding too patronising. The Three French Gentlemen had raised the same subject but, with all their experience and tact, could not help being condescending about another country's food. Where they failed the boys succeeded. We talked about what they liked to eat in Spain and at home and food was obviously a subject very close to their hearts.

They had been given permission to camp in a small park at the edge of the town and the talk about food reminded them that meal time was approaching. Now that they would be taking a least one rest day it was unlikely that we would meet again before the end of the journey.

The three of us stood and shook hands formally.

"See you in Santiago." said the one in chains, in English.

"In Santiago." I replied and sat down again to lean against the pillar and watch them leave the square the way they had come.

The traditional pilgrim dress of heavy cloak and broad-brimmed hat with its scallop shell badge has changed over the centuries. The shell is still the badge of the pilgrim on foot but the dress is now that of the walker. Some rich pilgrims of old would have brought their fine clothes with them. Modern pilgrims travelling by coach or car no doubt would be accompanied by an amount of luggage that would make sense of the Latin word for it, impedimenta.

However, I doubted that amongst their fashionable outfits, for every possible occasion, there would be any clothes more likely to achieve the desired attention in Santiago than my young friend's candy striped trousers and swinging, jangling chains and ear rings.

I could hear already his nailed boots clattering across the paving stones in front of the Apostle's Basilica.

The same staff were still on duty at the inn and working hard to keep up with the demands of the customers. In the dining room not all the tables had been cleared but one had been laid for me and I sat down with a view of the square.

Tired as they were, the staff excelled themselves with a fine meal, well cooked and served with courtesy and efficiency. The new, old town of Portomarin slipped quietly from evening to bright, starlit night. The Postada was another good resting place on the Camino.

CHAPTER 16

The Last Stage

The yellow arrows pointed towards another range of hills, the Montes de Valcaloura. All morning I climbed through forests and across open hillside, pleased to be off the surfaced road. The village of Hospital belied its name, being without sign of shop or café and having a large noisy pack of dogs to guard it. The locals saw the dogs massing for the stranger and very kindly intervened. I had second, and more well disposed thoughts towards the village.

The route crossed a main road and followed the line of a forestry road, still being constructed, towards the crest of the ridge. The foundations had been laid, flinty rocks crushed together by some giant roller. The trees and bushes on either side were so dense that I had to walk on the unmade road and it was most uncomfortable going. Then I reached the part which had been surfaced with fine chippings and powdered rock and, although it was very dusty, it was a great deal easier underfoot.

The day was very hot, but higher up there was cool air and very welcome shade. Underneath the tiredness of that day's journey was a deeper feeling of the weariness of almost continual travelling for over a month.

It was now less than a hundred kilometres to Santiago and I reckoned that three more days would see me there.

A walled laneway led into the village of Ligonde and for the first time I saw the narrow, slatted granaries perched on stone pillars. These are the Galician hórreos, built for the storage of maize and placed on pillars with tops like mushrooms to prevent the rats from taking their toll. The roof is steeply pitched, with a cross at one end and a carving, in this area usually a pyramid, at the other. One elegant hórreo, across two tall gate pillars, formed the archway of the entrance to a farm yard. The laneway was lined with hórreos and every one seemed to have the scallop shell carved on its side.

Each afternoon now felt hotter than the one before and I reached Palas de Rey tired and thirsty. I asked a woman for directions to the inn and she pointed across the street.

"Ahí está." she said, "There it is." She spoke very distinctly for the benefit of the stranger. I followed her pointing finger but could see no indication that any of the buildings was an inn. She stood watching me as I crossed to look. There was still no sign of the inn and I turned back to show my puzzlement.

"El auto verde!" she shouted, "The green car!"

I pointed at a closed door without conviction. There was no indication that it might be the right one.

"Bueno." she roared, probably wondering how this traveller had managed to come so far when he was not smart enough to see the inn he was looking at.

The door opened to the touch so I waved my thanks to my guide across the street and entered. The hallway was bare and a flight of stairs led to a landing. I knocked with my knuckles on a glass panel. The door was opened by a small woman dressed in black. She had a kindly look and was not in the least surprised to find a stranger on her first floor landing.

I asked the obvious question and she agreed that this was indeed the fonda. In a few moments I was installed in a small comfortable room. The bed was a double and the room just big enough to accommodate it. The window opened on to a yard and the atmosphere was calm, cool and airy.

The woman knew, without asking, that I was walking the pilgrim way and wondered if I would mind waiting to eight o'clock for dinner to allow her to go to mass. Having been used to waiting to a much later hour, I assured her that it suited me perfectly and went for my customary tour of the little town.

When I returned to the fonda at eight there was no sign of a dining room. I opened a door on the ground floor and looked into a bare, barn-like room with bicycles parked along one wall and a pile of boxes in a corner. I was about to retreat when instinct, or curiosity, told me to look further.

Once inside I could see that this might well be the dining room. Along the wall behind the door were two trestle tables, without table cloths but laid for a meal. The woman of the house entered from the kitchen and beckoned to me to sit down.

At some time in the past, this had been a fine, important room. At the far end was a curved bar counter of solid wood now dust covered and littered with discarded wrapping paper and pieces of twine. Behind it, attached to the wall, was a wooden arch of classical proportions. It had small ledges fitted to the curves each holding a dust-coated bottle. In another corner was an angled shelf at head height. It was stacked with supplies of soap, toilet rolls and packets of salt.

Hórreo in Galacia.

Hórreos are small barns raised on posts or stone piles to keep out the vermin and damp. They are used for storing maize and their construction and decoration varies from village to village. Most have slatted wooden sides, some are slated or tiles, others thatched. The scallop shell emblem appears on many along the route. One impressive Hórreo was perched across the massive gate pillars at the entrance to a farm yard.

I looked up and the ceiling was new. Thin, clean strips of pine had been fitted together with precision. Was this the first stage of the re-furbishing of the inn? I would have liked to ask but feared that the question might seem like a criticism of the room in its present state.

The laid tables were proof, that in the midst of the debris, the place was still in business and the ceiling a sign that someone felt it had a future.

The first course was a large tureen of soup set proudly before me and its name pronounced slowly so that I could understand.

"Caldo Gallego." The woman said and I repeated the words after her until she was satisfied that I had got the sound right. She explained that this was one of the special dishes of Galicia and very suitable for a traveller like me.

She brought a great round loaf to the table and a sharp knife as big as a small sword.

"Mire!" she said "Look! I will show you how to cut bread."

She held the loaf firmly against her apron and carved a thick slice, pulling the knife across the loaf parallel to her body. She set the loaf on the table and stuck the knife in the bread with enough force to stab it through to the wood.

The wine was served in an earthenware jug which was replenished every time I filled my glass.

"Do you like it? she asked and when I smiled and raised my glass to her she said, "It is our own."

The main course was steak served with salad and potatoes fried in the juices of the meat until they were crisp and delicious. By the time the next course was served I was ready to show that I could carve the bread. The woman watched closely as I demonstrated with as much style as I could muster.

"Hombre! Hombre!" she said laughing and shaking her head as she collected the empty dishes.

At the other table her family were having their meal and they included me in the company with gestures and smiles and without wanting to intrude. A girl of about twelve or thirteen arrived to visit and she was made welcome with great courtesy and charm.

It was a feeling of privilege to share the hospitality of this room. The present dilapidated state of it seemed irrelevant. Of its grand past, a cheerful spirit remained. It was easy to believe that this had always been a happy room at a friendly, welcoming inn.

Next morning I left Palas de Rey at the same time as the early morning bus left for the city of Lugo. As it was about to leave a girl came rushing down the street carrying a plastic bag. The driver paused when he saw her and waited as she produced her best shoes from the bag and leaned against a wall to put them on. It was easy to guess that she had walked a fair distance into the town but now she was ready for the city. She cliketty-clacked across the pavement in her high-heel shoes with the smart ankle straps and stepped up into the bus, no doubt feeling like a new woman.

The bus turned one way and I turned another and followed the arrows along quiet country lanes. It was warm and close, pleasant walking for I was now well used to this level of heat.

In the very far distance was the rumble of road traffic. Nearer was the staccato beat of a tractor and close to the sounds of the woods, bird song, frog chatter and the flickering of the breeze in the leaves.

I sat down with my back against a tree and closed my eyes to listen. It was as if I was hearing these sounds for the first time. The effect was like meditation music and all the tension of rushing through life had now disappeared.

I opened my eyes and saw a dream landscape. Between the trees was a prospect of miles of countryside streaked with eddies of early morning mist and ridge behind low ridge as far as the eye could see. Looking to the east, and against the light, back along the way I had come, the landscape was fixed in sharp relief by the contrast of light and shade.

The lanes led to a farmed area and the hórreos were a different shape. It was obviously another traditional form and these were circular, made of wattle and thatched. Their frequency clearly indicated the importance of the maize crop in Galicia.

All day a thunderstorm threatened. The atmosphere was close and muggy. Wisps of grey mist formed and then cleared slowly as the sun's power worked on the vapour. In the distance the thunder crackled, coming nearer and bringing the heavy, black rain clouds with it.

I stopped for a rest on the outskirts of the old village of Furelos and to shelter from the first downpour. Under a large broad-leafed tree a seat had been shaped from a log and I sat down and watched the rain wash the village. When the shower was almost over two women passed on their way to the well. They returned with their buckets full and stopped to pass the time of day with the stranger. They told me proudly, and without prompting, that their village had a grand past and was an important stopping place on the Camino. I followed them over the ancient bridge, now restored and with its pedigree proclaimed on a plaque fixed to its side. Even the dogs were friendly in Furelos.

As I left the village the road sign had been changed roughly with black paint from the Castillian 'MELLID' to 'MELIDE', a small alteration but no doubt an important one in these parts. The yellow arrows pointed away from the surfaced road however and, as it had done all day, the Road to Santiago took its own line along country lanes and forest paths.

Melide is a busy market town at an important road junction. Bruno's list recommended a place to stay, a Bar/Restaurant with rooms and I found it with ease at the very centre of affairs. It was a stylish, friendly place, its bar doing good business at the end of the afternoon. At the front was a covered terrace over-looking the main thoroughfare and this was obviously the place to take coffee and watch the world go by. The rain had passed leaving the town clean and fresh. I sat in the shade on the smart terrace and joined the locals in the serious and absorbing contemplation of the street life of Melide.

Next morning the route left the main road on the outskirts of the town and wandered through a wonderful wood of eucalyptus trees. I realised that I had left my stick propped against the wall in the bedroom at the Bar/Restaurant. Although it was a totally unreasonable reaction, surrounded as I was by wood, I almost went back for it.

Since Astorga I had made sure to be armed each day with a stick. Usually I found one in the morning and abandoned it in a hedge at the end of the day. Some were long and whippy, others as thick as cudgels. One had been straight and as long as a proper pilgrim's staff and I had used it, as they did, for vaulting streams and boggy patches. However it had not been as strong as it looked, or possibly I had not been as light as I felt. It had snapped during one such athletic feat and left me sitting on a muddy bank with a short, stout stick in either hand like a pair of Irish shillelaghs.

How I walked with my stick depended on its length and shape and how I felt. On some days I had held it like a shepherd's staff and used it as a third leg. There were times when I carried it in my hand as a weapon. Occasionally I used it as a walking stick and swung it jauntily like a gentleman's cane. The one left behind in Melide had become my favourite and had been with me for days. It was a strong, thin beech branch standing as high as my shoulder.

The previous year I had met a young Frenchman in the Pyrenees. He had just finished his first mountain walk and proudly showed me his staff. We took a bus together out of the mountains and he refused to have his staff stowed in the luggage compartment in case it might be lost. I knew how he felt. I found myself another stick and tried it out on the brambles.

A path through a eucalyptus wood is the most agreeable of walking. There is good shade but the light penetrates, moving and flickering as the walker travels. The leaves shiver in the gentlest of breezes. The ground is easy underfoot. The scent is delicate and fresh. It is an atmosphere fit for a fairy story.

The road through the woods of Galicia.

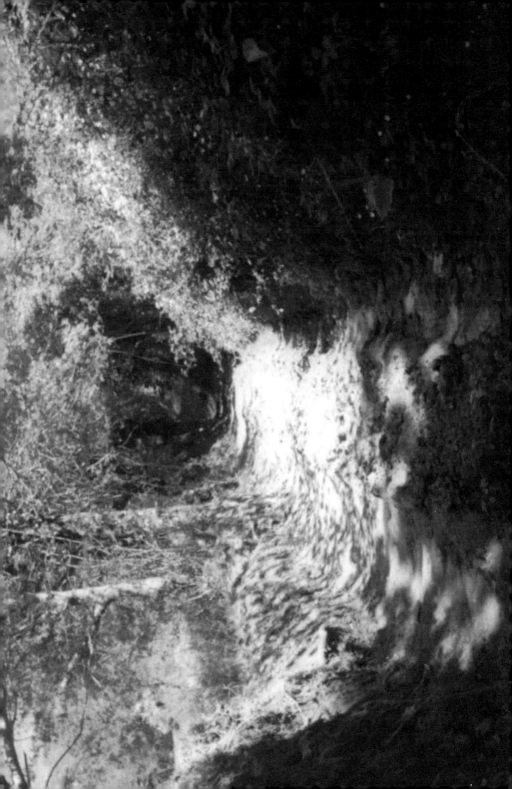

The eucalyptus bark regenerates itself, peeling as it grows, and is totally unsuitable for the painting of directional arrows. Even where the information seems vital, I find that signs on trees offend the eye. However I had been too long on the Camino and had been grateful often enough to those who had placed the signs, to be critical at this stage. A few days before I had missed an arrow almost peeled away on a eucalyptus trunk and had followed the track straight on instead of branching right. It had only meant a brief retreat back along a flooded and muddy lane but I wanted to tell the route markers about the eucalyptus bark. It peels!

For a brief space the route dumped me out on the main road and it was busy, noisy and very, very hot. It was a relief to turn off into a pine forest and follow a shady track with the traffic a low rumble in the distance. The walking was now so pleasant away from the road that I was beginning to resent each section, however short, on the highway.

Yesterday's thunderstorm had left the water lying on some parts of the track and there were places where its surface had been churned to deep mud by the passage of farm animals. It was obviously a recurring problem and it had been solved near a farm by a variation of the stepping-stones principle. Instead of stones carefully placed to step on, rounded mounds of hard mud had been constructed. The animals would have found the mud bumps as hard to negotiate as a cattle grid but, for a nimble human with a stick as an extra leg, it was easy to hop from lump to lump.

The names of the villages coincided with those on my map so it was a simple matter to keep a check on where I was. Earlier on the trip, it did not seem to be all that important but now I wanted to know. The villages I passed through were cheery, friendly places with a remarkable absence of dogs. At one hamlet there was only a small terrier to welcome me and he could bark and wag his tail at the same time, by way of fulfilling his duty to protect the property but also glad to see a friendly stranger.

Not for the first time, the yellow arrows were very erratically placed. Sometimes they appeared, as if by magic, when needed, clearly pointing the way. It was also possible to travel for three or four kilometres without any sign of an arrow, guessing at path junctions and trying to use the large scale map, which although useful as a guide for the general line of the route, did not show the paths. Santiago is almost due west of Melide and where there were no arrows I used the sun for direction. In the early morning I would be walking directly away from it, come the middle of the day it would be on my left hand and as the afternoon rays lengthened, they would be on my face.

I reached the small, pleasant town of Arzua, spotted a small inn at the road-side and sat down at a café in the main square for a cool drink. To have stopped here would have left over forty kilometres to Santiago on the last day. That would have meant arriving tired and late so I decided to walk on.

The route switched from the highway to forest paths and back again. But even the road was good walking as the traffic was so light. The distance slipped by bringing me closer to the end of the journey. After a pull up a steep little hill I crested a rise and walked down the long, late afternoon road into the sun. It was hot but not hot enough to make the sweat drip.

Ten kilometres beyond Arzua I reached the village of Ferreiros and was not surprised to find that there was no inn. A plan had already shaped itself in my mind. I remembered that the Belgian boys were allowed to leave the route by hitching a lift, provided that they came back to the same place to start walking again. So I turned and thumbed a lift back to the inn at Arzua intending to reverse the process next morning.

The inn at Arzua was called a hospederia and was tiny, a compact, friendly, neat and clean establishment with more staff than seemed necessary for such a small place. The bed rooms had little wrought-iron balconies just big enough to set my trainers on to air.

Shopping for food for the next day's journey the woman at the check-out at the grocery store realised that I was a foreigner. She called to her friend at the back of the shop to come to speak English to me. Her friend had worked in England and was glad of the chance to speak that language again. The pair of them plied me with questions on my travels, aware of the significance of the Road to Santiago but slightly puzzled that a foreigner should be on it.

I sat on a bench in a small park and, recognising me as a stranger, a group of young people came to talk to me. Their ages ranged from about nine to fourteen and we conversed in a curious mixture of English, Spanish and French which would have made their teachers squirm. They asked me my name and I became Alberto. They told me theirs, Juan, Ricardo, Teresa, Manuela, Carmen.

When they heard that I was walking they asked the obvious question. "Do you not have a car?" and when I said that I had, followed up with simple logic. "If you have a car, why are you walking?" There was nothing for it but the direct answer.

"Because I feel like it." I said and having translated the English amongst themselves, they nodded, accepting this as a good enough reason.

The young people were very curious about Ireland, particularly Northern Ireland. I turned the question back to them and their knowledge was a kaleidoscope of pictures from television news and fragments of school Geography lessons; the one disquieting, the other reassuring and both predictably so.

"Does it rain all the time in Ireland?" they asked. "Have you ever been bombed? Is it true that Ireland is the greenest country in the world? Do the people speak Irish in Ireland? Do you have a gun at home?": and then the crucial question to see which side I was on, "Are you Catholic or Protestant?"

This was not an interrogation, in adult fashion. The questions were without guile. They showed a real interest in the stranger, telling more than they asked, not necessarily needing to be answered directly. It was a salutary experience to see my country reflected in the bright eyes of these Spanish children.

The conversation changed quickly to television. They wanted to ask about the programmes which they could see here and which were also being shown on British and Irish T.V. I gathered that the current favourite in Arzua was the American soap opera Falcon Crest. They knew that the episodes being screened in Britain were further on in the story than those they were seeing and I was bombarded with questions about what would happen next. Sadly I was not able to help, knowing nothing about the programme save its name. They laughed and advised me to watch the series on my return.

"Good-bye Alberto." said Carmen in English when it was time for me to go. The others took it up as I walked away, "Good-bye Alberto."

It seems sad that in many parts of the world, and for very good reason, it would be regarded as a suspicious act for an adult stranger to sit and talk with a group of local children in a public park. The evil that some do demeans us all.

I turned to wave and heard one of the boys call "Alberto!". It was a shout of encouragement to carry me on my way.

When I returned to the inn I was asked into the kitchen to order my meal. Two large, jolly women were busy preparing the food, doing two or three things at a time, both ready to tell me about the menu. It was easy to predict that it would be a good meal. The raw ingredients were being prepared with care. The kitchen looked as if those who used it knew what they were about. The cooks themselves were happy at their work. I ordered and took my place at a window table.

By choice I was starting again with Caldo Gallego which, of course, could be a meal in itself. There are different traditional forms of this Galician speciality. Here it was made with white beans, bacon, pork, garlic sausage, potatoes and for me, the surprising ingredient of turnip tops. Bruno's advice had been that the pilgrim should have soup at the evening meal. At times he suffered from de-hydration and I had thought then that he meant that soup was a most suitable way to replace the liquid lost through sweating. Caldo Gallego would certainly do that but the substantial nature of its ingredients would assuage the hunger as well as the thirst. It was thus the ideal dish for the traveller on foot.

Next morning I was on the road at eight o'clock and hitched a lift without difficulty back to Ferreiros and to my stopping point on the previous evening. The yellow arrows took me away from the road and across country which seemed recently deserted by its people. Along the lane was a disused village school, windows cracked, the door hanging off its hinges. Inside, the blackboard was still on its easel, wiped clean and ready for use. The desks were in place, waiting for pupils. Since O Cebrero this was the fifth disused village school I had noticed. In the other areas I had felt that new schools must have been provided at the main road, each serving a larger area than the schools they replaced. Here the houses were empty too as if the people had drifted away and left the countryside empty.

This exodus from rural areas, in some countries once a sign of the hardest of times, is now a mark of the developing economy. People feel the need to be close to the new opportunities and diversions. What were once virtually unattainable luxuries are now the necessary conveniences of normal life. In spite of being more mobile, the countrypeople see their districts as being too remote. This place seemed deserted very recently and its emptiness gave it a dull and dismal air.

I crossed a bridge with a sign saying that it had been built by the Romans. Its origins were heavily concealed by modern repairs but I looked underneath and was impressed.

After the woods, lanes and little villages I came out on the road at the bottom of a long, steep slope. The road was recently constructed and rose in long sweeping bends cut into the surface of the land to leave steep, bare clay banks on either side. This new highway had been much needed for it was already heavily used by commercial traffic and private cars.

The heat came from two directions, from the sun directly above and upwards from the road surface like hot air from an electric convector heater.

At the crest of the ridge there was a new road junction and massive machines were pulling at the red earth, levelling it out for an extension to the airport which serves Santiago. All sign of the old route of the Camino had vanished.

The airport is called Labacolla after the village where the pilgrims stopped to wash before the last stage into Santiago itself. But this zone of earth movement was no place for a traveller to linger so I plodded on, feeling the heat and the whole of the distance since France.

Around a corner was a newly-built road-side restaurant. The parking space was almost full of smart cars and inside there was piped music. It was crowded but cooler than outside and I ordered a cold drink and a coffee at the bar counter. I took them to a corner table and in my sweaty, dusty state did my best not to lower the tone of the establishment.

At the next table an affluent Spanish family was having the kind of row which they hope no one else will notice. One of the sons, about eleven or twelve years old, was refusing to eat the lunch which had been served. The food looked interesting and appetising but he wanted Coca-Cola and potato crisps.

The father was scolding, as quietly as anger would allow and the mother was taking her son's part. Inevitably the boy resorted to tears and fled to the lavatory.

The wife turned on her husband, her voice low but as sharp as a two-edged fighting sword. He said nothing but looked at her without blinking, matching her words with silent rage.

When I stepped forward to the bar to pay, the man behind the counter held out his hand instead of a bill. We shook hands.

"There is no charge." he said in Spanish and then added in English, "Your trip to Santiago will be better than theirs.", nodding at the squabbling family and laughing without any hint of malice.

A wave of heat met me at the door but the next stretch was downhill and I had now less than ten kilometres to go.

At the village of San Marco the yellow arrows appeared again and I took the ancient route up the hill of Monte del Gozo to the place where, by tradition, the pilgrims had their first sight of Santiago de Compostela. At the crest young trees now block the view. Then I was clear of the wood and could see the city spread out before me. It was much bigger than I had imagined, its heart well set between the hills, its extremities straggling untidily out into the countryside.

I walked down the hill and into the Pilgrim City.

Confusing modern streets led, I suspected circuitously, to the older part and through a maze of narrow alleys I came out in a huge square, the Plaza del Obradoiro in front of the Cathedral.

The feast day of St. James, on the 25 July, was still two weeks away but the scaffolding, to provide staged seating and to suspend huge drapes, was already being erected.

An exhausted walker trudges along with slumped back and feet hitting the ground seemingly out of control. One who is merely very tired treads lightly, hoping to save the full weight from the feet, trying to keep balanced and erect.

I remembered a description of myself when I was a young teacher. It had been written by a thirteen year old who had been graded by the educational psychologist, much to the annoyance of the school's headmaster, as 'educationally sub-normal'. In an assignment for a colleague she had written, "Mr Slader is very jokey. He walks like a cat."

A little shop, no more than a hole in the wall, sold its own hand-made boots and shoes. Around the arch of the door hung the samples, a stout black shoe, a fine soft leather boot, a pair of wooden clogs and a knee-high Wellington boot with a wooden sole. Inside, an elderly man in a leather apron was carving a strip from a cured hide.

Next door was a bakery, advertised by a huge, circular loaf as big as a dust bin lid and with the surface worked in segments to a circular, crusty knob at its centre.

I heard the clamour of a single voice above the babble of buying and selling and went to investigate. A gipsy woman, with a voice that carried like a muezzin's from a minaret, was selling clothes from a multi-coloured pile dumped on a blanket on the pavement. She was the build of an opera contralto with black hair, gold teeth and both arms raised to her audience. She tossed her head and flashed her teeth. Her heels rattled on the pavement as she stamped and roared out in praise of her wares. Her public crowded around like the fans of a flamenco dancer, enjoying the entertainment, some even wanting to buy. Was she Mary Gipsy in a crimplene dress?

I went back to the cathedral and climbed the steps again to the Portal of Glory. Its columns are beautifully worked in marble by a master sculptor of the 12th century. Near the base of the central column are five holes which fit the fingers and thumb of the right hand. Over the centuries the marble has been worn by the touch of pilgrims' hands, as the bed-rock of the hills crossed by the Camino has been worn by their feet.

I waited while a mother held a child steady and the small hand stretched to fit the indentations. The tradition is, that with the hand in place, the pilgrim asks for a special blessing and that St. James will grant it to those who ask with sufficient fervour.

When it was my turn, I found the holes so deep that for a moment my hand seemed attached to the pillar.

At special masses a talent for the dramatic is revealed at the Cathedral. A huge silver censer, the Botafumerio, is hoisted aloft on a hemp rope pulled by eight men. Skilfully the censer is caused to swing back and forth over the heads of the worshippers. The crowd gasps, the charcoal sparks fly and the colossal urn sweeps down from the ceiling and skims the heads of the congregation below. The origin of this custom dates back to the 12th century. In the Codex Calixtinus it is somewhat mundanely explained that the Botafumerio was installed to swing through the transept to purify the air fouled by the smell of the thousands of pilgrims who stayed in the cathedral day and night.

Pilgrims who have walked to Santiago present themselves to the Cathedral Secretary to obtain a certificate of pilgrimage, unchanged

since medieval times and known as 'the Compostela'. The proof of the journey is the pilgrim's pass which should be stamped by the local priest at the over-night stopping places. I had not heard of the need for such a record before starting on the journey. It was my lack of one which had caused Bruno such concern. The office is in a remote corner of the Cathedral building and for the second time I found it closed.

The guided tour business was in full operation, each guide carefully shepherding his or her own flock, speaking the appropriate language, expounding history, tradition and religion in the manner of the infallible. The voices of the guides droned above the chatter as their charges shuffled and clattered around taking photographs against every possible background, presumably as evidence that they had, in fact, been here.

I sat down in a pew and the noise which, a moment before, had seemed so loud was no more than a reverential hum. Now the journey was over I was expecting a feeling of anti-climax. However, the sense of purpose which I had been aware of on the previous evening was still to the fore.

Impressions of the people and places of the journey flitted through my mind. At the beginning it had been a surprise to find that there were still a few pilgrims travelling on foot. After a few days the scale of the journey had impressed itself on me. It had been across the full width of Iberia. The physical effort had been ever-present. However it was also by-the-way, a part of the travelling, not some notable achievement in itself.

The long distance runner easily becomes obsessed by distance and time. I was glad that, having the advantage of being an indifferent runner over any distance longer than a sports pitch, there had never been a temptation to fall into those traps. Mountaineers and long distance walkers are equally vulnerable and need to guard against striving for the same false goals. Achieving so far in a day can seem so important that it becomes an end in itself. The pilgrim should have the benefit of sounder ambitions.

After the first few days of the journey my appreciation of the character of the Camino had developed steadily. This had happened through staying at villages like Puente la Reina, through meeting Bruno, the real pilgrim and by crossing remote tracks of countryside like the Meseta and the hills of Monte Irago.

At times it felt as if I was tramping through scenes in a medieval play, the drama of the people and places unfolding around me as I moved across the stage. The village streets, the old town houses, the castles and churches were all part of the set. The forests, the farmland and the mountains were the backdrops. In places, like Viana, the local people were the players, and there I had joined them in the play.

The covered market at Santiago.

The wooden pew was such a restful seat that it might have been designed to fit me and I wondered why there was an idea in my mind that church seats are always, and as if by intention, uncomfortable. Could it be that they are good enough seats if the sitter is ready for sitting there?

A large party of French pilgrims drifted down the aisle to see the altar close to. Their hub-bub roused me from my reverie as if they meant to have their presence noticed like loud conversationalists in a restaurant. The party split into small groups but surged together again, each member apparently afraid of becoming detached.

I thought of the loneliness I had felt over the first few days and remembered the same kind of ache when I had been a home-sick, nine-year-old evacuee at the beginning of the last World War.

It was not as if I was unused to travelling on my own. Walking alone felt the right way for me to travel, whether it was through settlements or across country empty of people. It was easier to set my own pace, to rest when I felt like it. It left me time to think and created a degree of awareness of people and places that I was sure I would have missed had I been accompanied.

The loneliness had made its mark at two times of the day only—when I stopped for rest and food in the middle of the day, and in the evening when it seemed that I might be the only one in the dining room at the inn. Then, as I settled to the journey, the loneliness had slipped away as stealthily as it had come.

The days on my own had allowed time to think, time free from the usual interruptions of life, the constant stream of messages with which we are bombarded and to which we are expected to respond. It also meant that there was nowhere to hide from the disquieting thought. Normally there is an easy way to avoid thinking about the uncomfortable. There are always those letters which need to be written, a telephone call to be made, a chore to be done, a friend or business colleague to be talked to, or a handy diversion by way of a television programme that must be seen.

In the bright, fresh air of the open road and in the calm, atmospheric light of churches, there had been time for me to consider my beliefs.

I left the Cathedral in cheerful, optimistic mood, the spirit calm, the mind alive and the body almost energetic. I could now match Santiago's liveliness with my own and joined the throng of local people, pilgrims and tourists on the streets of the Apostle's city. At pavement cafés the best seats, for watching the world walk by, were in great demand.

In the evening the visitors joined in the Spanish tradition of strolling as if they had been at it all their lives.

Starting out on the journey I had been the same weight as I was in my middle twenties. Here at its end I found a chemist's shop where there were old-fashioned scales of the type used to weigh boxers before a fight. The chemist himself slid the weights along the bar and I found I was lighter than I had been since my late teens.

I walked back to the Plaza del Obradoiro which creates the grand space in front of the Cathedral and thus enables it to be seen properly. At one side is The Hostal de los Reyes Cathólicos. It was founded by Ferdinand and Isabella as a pilgrim inn and has now been converted into a luxury hotel. As with the Paradors the hotel is proof of the special talent of the Spanish for the restoration and refurbishing of ancient buildings to a practical modern use.

The facade of the Hostal is memorable and its presence perfectly complements the Cathedral. Each provides the ideal vantage point for viewing the other. Inside the Hostal there was an atmosphere of charm and opulence. The furniture and hangings were exquisite, the staff numerous, discreet, courteous and efficient.

The Hostal's clientele is now the wealthy, on business, tourism, or pilgrimage. By tradition the pilgrim who has made the journey on foot or by bicycle is given either lunch or dinner at the hotel for three days without charge, on the production of the Compostela, the certificate of pilgrimage obtained from the Cathedral Secretariat. Bruno had told me that he intended to claim his free meals when he arrived, as he had done the previous year when he had made the journey by bicycle. I tried to picture him entering the elegant foyer of the Inn of the Catholic Monarchs and wondered if the hotel staff had given him the welcome that Ferdinand and Isabella would surely have insisted was his by privilege. I learned later that the free meals for pilgrims were not served in the hotel dining room but in the staff quarters. Would Los Reyes Cathólicos have approved?

The next morning I went back to the Cathedral to see if the pilgrims' office was open. The old man checking tickets at the wrought iron gate which led to the cloisters let me through, as usual grudgingly. The office was closed. On my return to the gate the old man was examining the visitors' tickets in his irascible fashion, letting a queue form. He looked up and stared at me without word or expression of recognition even though this was the third day on which we had met. But real help is in the act, not the gesture.

"¿Está cerrado?", "Is it closed?" He seemed to say.

I nodded. He closed the ledger with a snap, locked the cash box and leaving his queue standing, beckoned me to follow. He led the way through a maze of corridors into the very heart of the building, pushed open a door without knocking and was gone before I could thank him.

Inside was a room as big as a servants hall at a castle and similar in appearance and decor. Behind a wooden table was the cleric responsible for Compostelas. His greeting was quietly formal and he examined me with a sharp experienced eye. He began to interrogate me in Spanish, head down over his papers, each question on the heels of my stumbling answers. The few words that I had of his language slipped away from me like young eels through the fingers.

"What is your name? Where did you start your pilgrimage? How many days have you been on the road? When did you arrive in Santiago? Why have you not come for your Compostela for three days?"

A long time ago the Spanish made their name in the interrogation business with their version of the Inquisition. I hoped that this fine young cleric was not a Dominican with pretensions to the fame of Torquemada, a member of that order whose zeal earned him the title of the Grand Inquisitor.

He looked up and almost smiled by way of apology. He held out a hand and asked for something I did not have to give.

"Your pilgrim pass please." he said.

I tried to explain that before leaving I had not heard of the pass or the societies which will provide it for pilgrims. He was not able to understand my pidgin Spanish so I tried again. His look remained blank.

"Please, your pilgrim pass." he said, " I must see it."

"I have no pass." I said lamely, "I did not know I had need of one." I sounded like the lost soul in the hell-fire preacher's sermon crying out when it was too late, "I did not know Lord, I did not know."

At last he understood and stared at me with eyebrows raised, shaken by the seriousness of the revelation.

I decided to come clean.

"I am not a Catholic." I said, trying to say it without apology or belligerence and finding it hard to catch the right inflection. He nodded and suddenly thought of another question.

"Which country do you come from?" he asked.

"I am from Northern Ireland" I said trying again for the neutral tone. The weight of these last two items of information tipped the balance. He stood up to shake hands and smiled broadly.

"Welcome to Santiago." he said warmly. "Welcome to Spain."

I waited while he wrote my name on a parchment scroll. He rose again and formally presented it with a blessing.

"God be with you." he said in English.

For a few moments we chatted and I was amazed to find that he spoke that language clearly and accurately. By the time we parted I was sorry for having cast him in the role of a latter-day Torquemada sent to try me for heresy by default.

I left the Cathedral by the Portal of Glory, clutching my Compostela as if its possession was as vital to me as it would be to the boys from Belgium. I looked across at the Inn of the Catholic Monarchs. By custom they now owed me three free meals but, grateful as I was for that generous possibility, I decided to leave the debt uncollected.

The day was bright and hot and the good-natured crowd went about their business, pleasure or worship without knowing or even wondering why I felt so happy. Why should they? Each person's pilgrimage is their own life's journey.

In the days when he lived close to nature, the North American Indian brave tried to walk in the sacred manner. The medieval pilgrim would have approved. I felt that, in striving to do so too, I had stepped in some of their footprints.

> *On such a journey,*
> *As would make the head spin*
> *And set the sensibilities all awry.*
> *A journey back through time ,*
> *To feel the Road as they did*
> *And watch the distance trailing out behind,*
> *Like a gymnast's ribbon.*

APPENDIX 1

The first walk for the Multiple Sclerosis Society of Ireland (outside Ireland) was in 1989. This was along the Loire Valley to Paris. It was a great success and we were proposing to do something similar the following year - but to where? We researched many options until Donncha O'Dulaing arrived into the office with a copy of "Pilgrims' Footsteps" in his hand. This was to be the beginning of a wonderful walk for the MS Society and we quickly, with Bert's help, planned our first walk along our beloved Camino. This year we are celebrating our 10th anniversary walk and we are delighted, and indeed honoured, that our dear friend, Bert, will be leading his 9th walk to Santiago, for the Society. Finding "Pilgrims' Footsteps" was the key to a really great success story for the Society and unique in that it is, by far, the longest-running and most popular charity walk. Bert too has been a wonderful friend to the MS Society, not only does he lead our walks so well but he has also created a greater awareness for Multiple Sclerosis through his many lectures, radio and television appearances. The walk is now a very important part of our annual calendar of events and has raised over £600,000 to help the Multiple Sclerosis Society of Ireland provide professional and voluntary based services, including respite care, counselling, information and community support services to some 5,000 people with MS and to an approximate 8,000 others who share their lives. It also enables the Society to continue to fund vital research in Irish hospitals and universities.

The Camino is magnetic and one must experience it to fully understand the joy which is shared along the ancient pathways to Santiago. We feel privileged to have such a wonderful group of loyal supporters, many returning year after year, and each with a common bond to raise money to help others. They have greatly enriched my life and the lives of many people throughout Ireland with Multiple Sclerosis.

Lorna Mitchell
The Multiple Sclerosis Society of Ireland

1990

1990 was the start of the Pilgrim's Way to Santiago and I was fortunate to be part of that group, and was well supported by two friends Clare and Kate [later to be called the 'Blessed Trinity' by Donncha]. We were very 'green' and over anxious about the walk. I tried to allay our fears by painting a very positive picture. I firmly believed that we would start each day by strolling along a leafy lane for a few hours until we reached the bus, which would be parked always by a sparkling stream to chill the wine and to refresh our feet. Lorna would pull down an awning to shade us from the mid-day sun and serve a delicious lunch. The reason why we were told to bring guitars would unfold, we would have gentle music at siesta time. Then we would change our clothes and amble off to the nearest town.

Well - I was so wrong!

Despite Donncha assuring us at regular intervals as we staggered up another hill - "It's all down hill from now on" we were exhausted. Yet it was a magical and enriching experience.

Seven walks later, we have hosts of new companions and the best joy of all - we have been promoted from being the Blessed Trinity to become "Bert's bag ladies"!

Frances Finn.

Kate Walsh says "I have really delightful memories of my first Camino in 1990. The people in the tiny villages were so friendly and each wished us "Buen Viaje" as we passed through their sleepy hamlets. But for me the most moving experience was at the Iron Cross - it's starkness and simplicity - standing high up on a colossal collection of stones left by pilgrims over many decades. Each "peregrino" laid a stone (most of us brought one from home) made a wish, said a prayer, remembered our family, friends, sponsors and most of all the people for whom we were walking."

1990

Gabrielle Allen	*Dublin*	Phyllis McCarthy	*Wexford*
Orna Banim	*Dublin*	Ursula McHugh	*Derry*
Sheila Behan	*Kildare*	Patricia McMahon	*Louth*
Jim Blewitt (R.I.P.)	*Cork*	Rosaleen McNamara	*Kildare*
Mary Boyd	*Dublin*	Jack Meany	*Dublin*
Anne Byrne	*Galway*	Dermod Morrissy Murphy	*Limerick*
Laureen Callaghan	*Dublin*	Mary Morrissy Murphy	*Limerick*
Joy Casey	*Dublin*	Sadie Moynihan	*Waterford*
Jenny Clavin	*Galway*	Frank Muldowney	*Dublin*
Helen Corbett	*Kildare*	Kay Mullane	*Dublin*
Alan Coughlin	*Cork*	Theresa Mulleady	*Roscommon*
Gay Curran	*Dublin*	William Mullen	*Dublin*
Gerard Davis	*Dublin*	Dan Murphy	*Wicklow*
Jennifer Deegan	*Dublin*	Niamh Ní Fhloinn	*Dublin*
Sharon Devaney	*Donegal*	Patsy O'Brien	*Limerick*
Imelda Duffy	*Galway*	Brian O'Brien	*Cork*
Jo Egan	*Dublin*	Rory O'Connor	*Dublin*
Irene Fieghan	*Dublin*	Michael O'Driscoll	*Cork*
Frances Finn	*Cork*	Michael O'Leary	*Dublin*
Adam Grennan	*Dublin*	Aisling O'Neill	*Dublin*
Grainne Grennan	*Dublin*	Rev. O'Neill	*Dublin*
Deirdre Hamilton	*Dublin*	John O'Rourke	*Kilkenny*
Margaret Heffernan	*Sligo*	Mairead O'Sullivan	*Dublin*
Margaret Henihan	*Dublin*	Alice Parsons	*Galway*
Ian Hicks	*England*	Margaret Phelan	*Kilkenny*
Mary Howlett	*Dublin*	Mary Ryan	*Galway*
Tom Huban	*Galway*	Mary Ryan	*Waterford*
Michael Kilduff	*Kildare*	Mary Seale	*Galway*
Bernie Lee	*Dublin*	Mary Shannon	*Cork*
Brid Leo	*Galway*	Seamus Smith	*Dublin*
Jean Maguire	*Meath*	Paul Sweeney	*Dublin*
Brian Mannion	*Galway*	Catherine Sweeney	*Dublin*
Patsy Marnane	*Tipperary*	Caitlin Ui Flannagain	*Dublin*
Phil McCarthy	*Cork*	Kate Walsh	*Cork*

1991

For ***Tom Huban*** the highlights for 1991 were:
"The impromptu concert on the streets of the tiny village of Ledigos, with Frank Muldowney 'doing' Bert and Lorna conducting "How Great Thou Art" in preparation for our visit to the cathedral. I remember too

the villagers, all 20 of them, peeping shyly around the street corners to see what was happening in their sleepy village. We did, however, manage to persuade a mother and daughter to give us a song in Spanish about the Camino - it was lovely. We ended up dancing, along with the villagers in the streets which for too long had been sadly deserted.

Bodegas Riojanes provided a welcome break where the rioja wine flowed and the meatballs were not what they seemed!! The walking was tough, the weather very hot and our arrival at the square in Santiago was filled with hugs and kisses and a great feeling of 'we did it'. To crown it all I will never forget the sound of Irish voices singing "Céad míle fáilte romhat a Íosa" in the magnificent Cathedral in Santiago."

1991

Jim Blewitt (R.I.P.)	Cork	Susan Mahony	Cork
Geraldine Candon	Dublin	Jim McClatchie	Dublin
Joy Casey	Dublin	Jack McLoughlin	Tyrone
Mamie Clark	Donegal	Mary McNulty	Down
James Conlon	Dublin	Robert McNulty	Galway
Denise Conn	Dublin	Margaret Monaghan	Donegal
Helen Corbett	Kildare	Dermod Morrissy Murphy	Limerick
Veronica Delaney	Dublin	Mary Morrissy Murphy	Limerick
Carmel Dempsey	Galway	Frank Muldowney	Dublin
Noreen Dennihy	Tipperary	Dan Murphy	Wicklow
Clare Dollard	Dublin	John P. Murphy	Dublin
Tom Ewing	Dublin	Niamh Ní Fhloinn	Dublin
Miriam Foley	Dublin	Brian O'Brien	Cork
Rose Anne Foley	Cork	Pakie O'Callaghan	Cork
Vivienne Foley	Sligo	Gerard O'Donnell	Mayo
Denis Gill	Dublin	Eileen O'Neill	Dublin
Paddy Hackett	Dublin	Maura O'Neill	Dublin
Don Henihan	Dublin	Michael O'Neill	Dublin
Ray Hennessy	Cork	Frances O'Reilly	Dublin
Pat Hickey	Clare	Michael O'Reilly	Dublin
Dick Hogan	Cork	Margaret Parle Caulfield	Wexford
Mairead Holten	Meath	Linda Perle	England
Tom Huban	Galway	Helen Power	Dublin
Marie Hughes	Antrim	Deirdre Quinlan	Dublin
Robert Hyland	Dublin	Irene Quinn	Dublin
Martin Jennings	Mayo	Colette Reilly	Dublin
Seamus King	Down	Gerry Ryan	Mayo
Deirdre Lillis	Dublin	Michael Ryder	Mayo
John Lindsay	Dublin	Marie Turner O'Brien	Dublin
Mary Mahony	Cork	Clare Whelan	Kildare

1992

The Camino '92 was certainly one to remember, not just because of the seven days on which it rained but more for the camaraderie of the people who shared this wonderful Camino. The walking was tough particularly the day we walked to Castrojeriz when the mud clung to our boots and refused to be shaken off as we slip-slod our way along the little pathways. That day too we were absolutely drenched arriving at the bus for lunch. We had a bite to eat, a change of clothes and a few words from Bert convinced us that "things weren't too bad at all" and so we were off again to complete the day's journey.

Improvisation was the key. Black refuse sacks were transformed into the trendiest looking wet gear which gave the walkers the look of a macabre fancy-dress parade! The rain did not dampen our spirits and singing broke out from time to time (often lead by our dear friend the late Jim Blewitt) which gave us great encouragement to keep going and the sense of achievement on reaching Santiago all the greater. Our walking companion Fr. Jack Lynch said mass in the Cathedral, and there we had time to reflect on many aspects of life and most of all to think about the people for whom we made the journey. The rain was insignificant!

Mick Linehan

1992

Susan Bayne	*Cork*	Angela Harmon	*Wicklow*
Michael Blake	*Clare*	Pat Hickey	*Clare*
Jim Blewitt (R.I.P.)	*Cork*	Dick Hogan	*Cork*
Marie Brennan	*Dublin*	Dorothy Johnson	*Dublin*
Anne Carpenter	*Wicklow*	Roger Kennedy	*Dublin*
Marie Donnelly	*Dublin*	Michael Linehan	*Laois*
Frank Down	*Dublin*	Jack Lynch	*Dublin*
Jo Egan	*Dublin*	Daniel MacGowan	*Dublin*
Geraldine Fahy	*Dublin*	Jean Maguire	*Meath*
Frances Finn	*Cork*	Mick McLoughlin	*Dublin*
Rose Anne Foley	*Cork*	Audrey McVey	*Dublin*
Ann Gallagher	*Tipperary*	Gerald McVey	Dublin
Jennifer A. Gartlan	*Down*	Sheila Meehan	*Donegal*
Vonnie Goulding	*Dublin*	Bernie Moore	*Meath*
Louise Graham	*Dublin*	Frank Muldowney	*Dublin*
Dolores Grant	*Dublin*	William Mullen	*Dublin*
Malcolm Grant	*Waterford*	Kevin Murnaghan (R.I.P.)	*Tyrone*

Nuala Murnaghan	*Tyrone*	Jackie Regan	*Cork*
Marie Murphy	*Kerry*	Vincent Reilly	*Dublin*
Declan Nutley	*Louth*	Lorraine Rooney	*Dublin*
Niamh Ní Fhloinn	*Dublin*	John J. Ryan	*Wicklow*
Eileen O'Connor	*Dublin*	Mary Shannon	*Cork*
Liam O'Gallcobhair	*Tipperary*	Sheila Thomson	*Dublin*
Tony O'Neill	*Dublin*	Pauline Tierney	*Dublin*
Anne O'Riordan	*Dublin*	Kevin Tunney	*Dublin*
Padraig O'Siochru	*Dublin*	Brinain Vickers	*Dublin*
Toni O'Sullivan	*Cork*	Kate Walsh	*Cork*
Ruth Potterton	*Dublin*	Anne Walshe	*Dublin*
Mary Power	*Cork*	Joan White	*Dublin*

1993

The day we walk up O Cebreiro is always a very special day. It's the one day we break up into different groups, giving everyone a chance to reach the top at their own chosen speed. Group One normally comprises of the fast walkers of the group, those wishing to reach O Cebreiro as quickly as possible with little or no stopping and May 25th 1993 was no exception. The first group limbered up and were rearin' to go and disappeared into the distance at practically a run. We were in Group Two, and after about ten minutes or so we set off at our own slower pace.

We had been walking for some time when we heard shouts from behind and you can imagine our amazement when we turned to find Group One running up behind us, as we would have expected them to be at least half way to the top at this stage. It was very funny, we all stood to one side and clapped as they went by, all very red faced, but it would be fair to say that it was from the heat and not from embarrassment at having taken a wrong turn!! Suffice to say they did reach the top well before the rest of us, but their victory was somewhat tainted by our pleasure at their obvious mistake, though needless to say they maintained that the walk was too short for their capabilities and they were only trying to lengthen it. But we knew better!!!

Jean Maguire & Lorraine Rooney

Mary Shannon remembers that day well -

"I still laugh about this day as I had opted to go with the first group to make the ascent to O Cebreiro. Two of the leaders of our small group of about eight took off at a gallop and all was going well 'til our path came to an abrupt end - to our horror we were on the wrong road!!

We were absolutely mortified having to turn back right behind the second group. We tried to be serious and pretend all was well but serious we could not remain when the second group stood back and clapped us through. Our two leaders decided the only way we could redeem ourselves was to practically run up to O Cebreiro. We arrived two hours ahead of the others, absolutely exhausted and asked ourselves was it worth it and believe it or not it the answer was - yes!!"

1993

Marita Barrow	*Cork*	Dick Hogan	*Cork*
Michael Blake	*Clare*	Joe Hore	*Wexford*
Jim Blewitt (R.I.P.)	*Cork*	Martin Jennings	*Mayo*
Bernadette Brennan	*Kilkenny*	Gary Jermyn	*Dublin*
Lucia Byrne	*Louth*	Ann Keating	*Dublin*
Eithne Cavanagh	*Dublin*	Ann Keddy	*Dublin*
Mamie Clark	*Donegal*	John Lawler	*Dublin*
Deirdre Connolly	*Kerry*	Deirdre Lillis	*Dublin*
Cora Corbett	*Dublin*	Michael Linehan	*Laois*
Gabriel Cribben	*Meath*	Jean Maguire	*Meath*
Ted Cronin	*Kerry*	Annette Mahon	*Dublin*
Siobhan de hOir	*Dublin*	Bryan McGennis	*Dublin*
Ray Doherty	*Cork*	Jack McLoughlin	*Tyrone*
Sheila Donlon	*Dublin*	Josephine McLoughlin	*Dublin*
Senan Doohan	*Dublin*	Paddy McLoughlin	*Dublin*
Jo Egan	*Dublin*	John Miller	*Dublin*
Frances Finn	*Cork*	Eileen Mogerley	*Dublin*
Trish Finnan	*Tipperary*	Len Montgomery	*Dublin*
Vivienne Fogarty	*Cork*	Frank Muldowney	*Dublin*
Rose Anne Foley	*Cork*	Dan Murphy	*Wicklow*
Ann Gallagher	*Tipperary*	Martin Murphy	*Wexford*
Colm Geary	*Derry*	Rosarie Murphy	*Cork*
Fionnuala Geary	*Derry*	Niamh Ní Fhloinn	*Dublin*
Dolores Grant	*Dublin*	Nuala Ní Dhomhnaill	*Dublin*
Angela Harmon	*Wicklow*	Donal O'Connor	*Kerry*
Nuala Healy	*Cork*	Liam O'Gallcobhair	*Tipperary*
Daphne Henderson	*Tipperary*	Michael O'Leary	*Dublin*
		Michael O'Neill	*Dublin*

Margaret Parle Caulfield	*Wexford*	Mary Rowley	*Dublin*
Ruth Potterton	*Dublin*	Mary Shannon	*Cork*
Maeve Quirke	*Dublin*	Margaret Shorten	*Cork*
Mary Quish	*Limerick*	Hal Sisk	*Kildare*
Josephine Robinson	*Dublin*	Rosemary Sweeney	*Galway*
Lorraine Rooney	*Dublin*	Kate Walsh	*Cork*

1994

Arriving at journey's end is always to be a significant moment but nothing could have prepared us for the Santiago we entered in 1994 after the wonders of ten days across the hills, plains, plateaux and mountains of northern Spain.

As we came down onto the main road from the Monte del Gozo, cars full of football supporters rocked past, blue and white scarves streaming. Today was the day that Santiago were to make an attempt on the First Division. Success had perpetually eluded them. This time they had a chance.

The local attitude to pilgrims may well run to a wide spectrum. However, in a curious way they are an emblem of the city, even if they inevitably must be from somewhere else. Horns sounded enthusiastically and supporters waved and cheered wildly as they passed us.

In the evening a small group of us rushed down empty streets to discover where Santiago's heart was. A huge crowd was crushed in front of a gigantic screen which had been installed in the aged surroundings. Not quite with it from so many experiences over the last few days, suddenly we were submerged in a sea of jubilant if very, very tense people.

The details of the game eluded us, but the result didn't and couldn't. About two minutes after we arrived in the Plaza the crowd erupted with jubilation and we were in the middle of it. For a moment, as people started to jump in the fountains and part of the crowd started to swirl and eddy, the police looked anxious. Then what might have spilled over into riot, eased and relaxed. We were befriended and taken in hand by some friendly local people and we made our way from the old part of the city into the more modern area. It seemed as if the whole of Santiago was out and embracing the carnival. Those who weren't filling the streets were leaning out of windows, cheering and throwing water out onto the crowd below.

Few parties are the uplifting occasions they claim to be. This was the biggest I was ever at and I have rarely experienced delight like it.

Julian Watson

1994

Terry Anderson	*Cork*	Kay Igoe	*Galway*
Brioni Barnes	*Dublin*	Fergus Jordan	*Dublin*
Louise Barrett	*Dublin*	Ellie Keating	*Galway*
Jim Blewitt (R.I.P.)	*Cork*	John Kilduff	*Kildare*
Susan Boyle	*Dublin*	Michael Linehan	*Laois*
Lorraine Brady-O'Leary	*Dublin*	Seamus MacAogain	*Westmeath*
Joan Byron	*Clare*	Dave Marriott	*Kerry*
Peter Carton	*Wexford*	Sylvia Meyers	*Dublin*
Catherine Cheatle	*Dublin*	Frank Muldowney	*Dublin*
Cora Corbett	*Dublin*	Denis Murphy (R.I.P.)	*Dublin*
Amanda Crawford	*Donegal*	Kay Murphy	*Clare*
Sandra Dalton	*Dublin*	Mary Murphy	*Dublin*
Roger Dowds	*Dublin*	Donal O'Brolchain	*Dublin*
Austin Durack	*Limerick*	Anne O'Byrne	*Dublin*
Linda Fitzgerald	*Dublin*	Enda O'Connor	*Galway*
Eilis Fitzsimons	*Down*	Derek O'Leary	*Dublin*
Dympna Funge	*Dublin*	Oliver Sammon	*Galway*
Paula Griffin	*Waterford*	Carol Anne Veale	*Dublin*
James Healy	*Kilkenny*	Aileen Walsh	*Cork*
Dick Hogan	*Cork*	Julian Watson	*Antrim*

1995

In expectancy, bundled against the wind and mist, we set out at 4,500 ft. Our path through the Pyrennees takes us through groves of mountain Oak and Beech. It is Spring, the buds have been unfolding, yet as so often happens bursts of January-like winds sear south from the Artic and burn and shrivel all in their path. So it was '95. Walking on with old and new friends, I reflected on our purpose - journeying for those strong souls blighted in their spring. Dropping below the cloud line Roncevalles appeared bathed in sunlight.

The Refugio at Rabanal is a back to front place. As its name suggests, it provides shelter and sustenance for travellers at the end of their day. Yet Bert traditionally uses this place as the start of a journey through the deserted land of the Muleteers of the Maragatos- past the Druidic Cruz de Ferro and on to the welcome of the inn at the Roman bridge of Molinaseca. Promoted by the UK Friends of St. James, this place has always afforded us a welcome. No more so than in '95 when in memory of Jim Blewitt, we presented a stained glass window.

Morning in Lugo, a look skyward suggested rain. Not unusual in Galicia and for the experienced pilgrim these would be ideal conditions. On this last day of walk, deep friendships have been cemented, and despite Lorna's admonitions, you tend to walk with a small group of soul mates Anam Chara. Some miles before Santiago you drop, then rise through a forest of 200 year old Eucalyptus trees. Bright sunlight, high wind, driving rain, and you will miss Nirvana. But in '95, the mists hung low, drops of water condensed on the high foliage, 100-year-old bark fell in shards from knarled tree trunks, and the scent was an Aromatherapists ecstasy.

The hand wash in Lavacolla removed but little and with people I hope to love for the rest of my mortal, we entered Santiago.

Malcolm J. Grant

1995

Gemma Allner Ellis	*Dublin*	
Patrick Bissett	*Dublin*	
Anne Bowes	*Dublin*	
Eva Maria Braun	*Germany*	
Ted Cashman	*Cork*	
Pat Caulfield	*England*	
Cora Corbett	*Dublin*	
Ann Cosgrove	*Longford*	
Gabriel Cribben	*Meath*	
Aly Cummins	*Dublin*	
Noelle Dineen	*Cork*	
Rosaleen Dowling	*Wexford*	
Jo Egan	*Dublin*	
Catriona Fallon	*Dublin*	
Vonnie Goulding	*Dublin*	
Malcolm Grant	*Waterford*	
Tommy Hanratty	*Dublin*	
Anne Hassett	*Wicklow*	
Dick Hogan	*Cork*	
Tom Huban	*Galway*	
Ellie Keating	*Galway*	
Rosemary Leeson	*Wicklow*	
Michael Linehan	*Laois*	
Jean Maguire	*Meath*	
Bryan McGennis	*Dublin*	
David Mogerley	*Dublin*	
Len Montgomery	*Dublin*	

1995 cont'd.

Frank Muldowney	*Dublin*	Theresa Price	*Dublin*
Sean Murphy	*Dublin*	Maeve Quirke	*Dublin*
Aideen O'Brien	*Waterford*	Lorraine Rooney	*Dublin*
Enda O'Connor	*Galway*	Mary Shannon	*Cork*
June O'Connor	*Cork*	Bert Slader	*Down*
Ruth Potterton	*Dublin*	Gerry Smith	*Dublin*
Karen Price	*Dublin*	Aileen Walsh	*Cork*
Niamh Ní Fhloinn	*Dublin*	Norah Walshe	*Mayo*

1996

Memories, memories each year on the Camino with MS brings fresh experiences and new friends. Can one ever forget in 1996 meeting some of these characters: "my forever friend" Councillor John, Tommy with his healing hands especially for foot massages, Alex the exuberant architect whose sketches we all treasure, and being led into Santiago by John and Jean "the lesser" separated by some sixty years in age. We visited Euanate for the first time, a tiny jewel of a Church near Puente la Reina, and in the best tradition of so many churches along the Camino locked! On our way through Azofra we were almost swept up in the colourful procession of their Saint, saint Rita along the tiny streets of the village - another first!

In the best tradition of MS groups we also did a little bit of singing and perhaps nowhere more memorably than with the Poor Clares in their Convent at Castrojeriz. We went to early mass and during the service we were to sing "How Great Thou Art", our party piece, all one can say is that we tried, it was a disaster, until Lorna took a hand and rescued us, however not before we had highly entertained some of the nuns behind the grille who were seen to be in fits of laughter at our efforts.

We stamped all the Pilgrim Passports for the group and one memorable day we dashed ahead of the group into Boadilla, got the passports stamped and dashed out again expecting to catch the main group as we walked along the canal, but the group were nowhere to be seen so we almost ran to Fromista not knowing that Amanda had led the main group through the village and had made an ice-cream stop so in fact we were well ahead not behind,such are the hazards of stamping passports on the Camino!!

Bryan McGennis & Ruth Potterton

1996

Tara Andrews	*Waterford*
Patrick Barry	*Dublin*
John Costello	*Dublin*
Amanda Crawford	*Donegal*
Hanna Davis	*Kerry*
Patrick Dineen	*Spain*
Tommy Hanratty	*Dublin*
Angela Harmon	*Wicklow*
Michael Hayes	*Dublin*
Fergus Jordan	*Dublin*
Eileen Keaney	*Sligo*
Susan Keenan	*Wicklow*
Jean Kennedy	*Meath*
Joe Kennedy	*Tipperary*
Georgina Kenny	*Westmeath*
Rosemary Leeson	*Wicklow*
Michael Linehan	*Laois*
John Magan	*Longford*
Jean Maguire	*Meath*
Bryan McGennis	*Dublin*
Michelle Melotte	*Westmeath*
Jerry Moriarty	*Kerry*
Frank Muldowney	*Dublin*
Patrick Mullen	*Donegal*
William Mullen	*Dublin*
Niamh Ni Fhloinn	*Dublin*
John O'Halloran	*Dublin*
Siobhan O'Scanaill	*Dublin*
Ruth Potterton	*Dublin*
Mary Shannon	*Cork*
Patricia Swords	*Dublin*
Mary Tuite	*Dublin*
Carol Anne Veale	*Dublin*
Clodagh Veale	*Dublin*
Julian Watson	*Antrim*
Alex Whyte	*Cork*
Anna Whyte	*Cork*

Night of the Camino 1997

"On Raglan Road on an autumn day, I saw her first and knew".

The words of the poet Kavanagh sung loud and clear in a low hard bar in the shadow of the bridge at Puente la Reine. The timbre of Tom Huban's voice capturing one thousand years of tradition. His song echoing out on to the dark stones of the night street.

"On a quiet street where old ghosts meet, I see her walking now"

In Leon I stood with my ear pressed to the vast cathedral door listening to a full orchestra perform Beethoven's Mass. I looked outwards across the stone paving to where Austin Durack stood absorbed in the music. I looked upwards where the floodlit cream coloured stone of the cathedral was etched against the ink black of the night sky. Then I saw it. A small cloud of white ethereal snowflakes had appeared over Austin's head. A recognition from on high of this talented musician singer/songwriter's contribution to the lore of the Camino, perhaps!

I looked back up at the cathedral only to see the posterior of a stork protrude from the intricate carving. "Jump", I shouted! Austin jumped and the contents of the stork's bowel landed splat where he had just stood!

"When the angel woos the clay he'll lose his wings at the dawn of the day".

Alex & Anna Whyte

1997

Gemma Allner Ellis	*Dublin*	Michael Hayes	*Dublin*
Michael Blake	*Clare*	Maura Huban	*Galway*
Ray Brennan	*Mayo*	Tom Huban	*Galway*
Grainne Breslin	*Dublin*	Larry Joy	*Limerick*
Gerard Conlon	*Kildare*	Mairead Leahy	*Dublin*
John Costello	*Dublin*	Michael Linehan	*Laois*
Niamh Courtney	*Dublin*	Jean Maguire	*Meath*
Gabriel Cribben	*Meath*	Declan Mallen	*Wicklow*
Laura Curtis	*Dublin*	Sarah Mallen	*Wicklow*
Siobhan de hOir	*Dublin*	Bryan McGennis	*Dublin*
Eddie Deevy	*Waterford*	Jim McKenna	*Dublin*
Margaret Donohoe	*Dublin*	Siobhan McKenna	*Dublin*
Austin Durack	*Limerick*	Conor Montague	*Dublin*
Anne Forde	*Dublin*	Frank Muldowney	*Dublin*
Marion Gowan	*Wexford*	Niamh Ni Fhloinn	*Dublin*
Malcolm Grant	*Waterford*	Lorraine Rooney	*Dublin*
Donal Griffin	*Dublin*	Julian Watson	*Antrim*
Paddy Hackett	*Dublin*	Alex Whyte	*Cork*
Tommy Hanratty	*Dublin*	Anna Whyte	*Cork*

1998

"To be invited to add a few lines to this edition of Bert's book is a real delight. We have walked together in China, India and 1998 was my third year on the Camino, a special year with marvellous memories. This was the first year with a significant change to our usual route when we started in our beloved Pyrenees over what is known as the Somport Pass *(near a lovely old town called Jaca)*, in the early morning mist but happily finished in beautiful sunshine. The next two days in the Pyrenees were memorable, not just because of the beauty of the mountains, but we were treated to dreadful weather including a spectacular thunderstorm along the old Monks Pass!! The going was tough, the terraine rough but we finished that day in a little alpine hostelry and with steam rising from our wet clothes, we congratulated each other and toasted the end of a great day's walk by the log fires!

Bert's philosophy of "Enjoy the journey and the destination will look after itself" proved particularly apt when Sarah from Cavan and myself led the walk on the last day into Santiago. An interesting progression from wanderer to walker to pilgrim!"

1998

Tara Andrews	*Waterford*
Kathy Bateson	*England*
Sile Bennett	*Laois*
Kathleen Burke	*Dublin*
Desmond Campbell	*U.S.A.*
Martine Carlier-Lavery	*Clare*
Arlene Carroll	*Monaghan*
Jimmy Carroll	*Monaghan*
Valerie Casey	*Dublin*
Sarah Casserley	*Cavan*
Fiona Collins	*Cork*
John Costello	*Dublin*
Amanda Crawford	*Donegal*
Maureen Curtis	*Dublin*
Siobhan de hOir	*Dublin*
Patricia Donnelly	*Kildare*
Brendan Doran	*Laois*
Mary Dowling	*Dublin*
Breda Dreelan	*Dublin*
Anne Forde	*Dublin*
Mary Foyle	*Galway*
Jean Greene	*Dublin*
Aidan Grimes	*Louth*
Michael Hanna	*Dublin*
Patrick Hanna	*Dublin*
John Hayes	*Limerick*
Denise Hazley	*Dublin*
Marie Hegarty	*Donegal*

Patrick Hurley	*Limerick*
Jan Hyland	*Dublin*
Heather Kennedy	*Meath*
Mairead Leahy	*Dublin*
Michael Linehan	*Laois*
Jean Maguire	*Meath*
Hilary Marchant	*Dublin*
Bryan McGennis	*Dublin*
Donal McGrath	*Waterford*
Conor Montague	*Dublin*
Frances Nolan	*Wexford*
Moira O'Brien	*Monaghan*
Martha O'Byrne	*Dublin*
Frank O'Grady	*Dublin*
John O'Halloran	*Dublin*
Tim O'Leary	*Meath*
Michael O'Reilly	*Dublin*
Mary O'Shea	*Dublin*
Ruth Potterton	*Dublin*
Lorraine Rooney	*Dublin*
Pat Rooney	*Dublin*
Eamon Ryan	*Tipperary*
Mary Shannon	*Cork*
Tony Sheridan	*Dublin*
Rachel Treacy	*Carlow*
Kees Van Tergouw	*Wicklow*
Alex Whyte	*Cork.*
Mary Woods	*Meath*

1999

At the time of going to press the following people hope to join us for our 10th anniversary MS Walk to Santiago:-

1999

Anne Brophy	*Waterford*	Michael Linehan	*Laois*
Anthony Brophy	*Waterford*	Hilary Marchant	*Dublin*
Aidan Burke	*Dublin*	Mary McCann	*Galway*
Desmond Campbell	*U.S.A.*	Bernadette McCarthy	*Meath*
Gilly Carey	*Wicklow*	Bryan McGennis	*Dublin*
Valerie Casey	*Dublin*	Michael McHale	*Limerick*
John Costello	*Dublin*	Leo Mullen	*Dublin*
Maureen Curtis	*Dublin*	Margaret Nugent	*Meath*
Mary Dempsey	*Kildare*	June O'Connor	*Cork*
Denis John Downes	*Wexford*	John O'Halloran	*Dublin*
Breda Dreelan	*Dublin*	Tim O'Leary	*Meath*
Mary Foyle	*Galway*	Bill O'Neill	*Cork*
Maire George	*Carlow*	Myra O'Reilly	*Cork*
Malcolm Grant	*Waterford*	Rita O'Sullivan	*Meath*
Sinead Griffiths	*Dublin*	Hazel Perdue	*Dublin*
Sheila Hallinan	*Tipperary*	Ruth Potterton	*Dublin*
Martin Hanna	*Antrim*	Helen Power Quinn	*Dublin*
Michael Hanna	*Dublin*	Una Purcell	*Limerick*
Phil Hanna	*Dublin*	Michael Quinn	*Dublin*
Tara Hanna	*Antrim*	Hal Sisk	*Kildare*
Michael Hayes	*Dublin*	Sam Stephenson	*Kildare*
Maura Huban	*Galway*	Noreen Tracey	*Dublin*
Tom Huban	*Galway*	Kay Vaughan	*Clare*
Mary Hyland	*Dublin*	Gil Warnock	*Antrim*
Sheila Hynes	*Dublin*	Alex Whyte	*Cork*
Gerry Jones	*Monaghan*	Anna Whyte	*Cork*
Jo Keenan	*Dublin*	Mary Woods	*Meath*
Roger Kennedy	*Dublin*		